Chapter and Unit Tests
for English Language Learners and Special-Needs Students
with Answer Key

HOLT

World History
The Human Journey
Modern Era

HOLT, RINEHART AND WINSTON
A Harcourt Education Company
Austin • Orlando • Chicago • New York • Toronto • London • San Diego

Copyright © by Holt, Rinehart and Winston

Printed in the United States of America

ISBN 0-03-065736-9

07 08 09   018   08 07 06

Contents

Contents

CHAPTER **1**

Chapter Test Form C

The Emergence of Civilization

MATCHING *(3 points each)* Place the letters of the descriptions next to the appropriate terms.

_____ **1.** civilization

_____ **2.** artifacts

_____ **3.** domestication

_____ **4.** cultural diffusion

_____ **5.** Cro-Magnons

_____ **6.** agriculture

_____ **7.** culture

_____ **8.** Lucy

_____ **9.** irrigation

_____ **10.** hominids

a. the taming of animals such as cattle, goats, sheep, and pigs

b. a set of beliefs, knowledge, and patterns of living that a group of people develop

c. term used to describe humans as well as earlier humanlike creatures

d. name given to the hominid skeleton found in 1974 by Donald Johanson

e. *Homo sapiens* that appeared in Europe after the disappearance of the Neanderthals

f. the raising of crops for food

g. objects—such as tools, clothing, works of art, weapons, and toys—made and used by humans

h. a complex culture that has the ability to produce extra food; large cities or towns with some form of government; and people performing different jobs

i. a system for moving water from its source to a field for farming

j. the spread of ideas and other aspects of a culture from one area to another

FILL IN THE BLANK *(3 points each)* Choose from the following list to complete each of the statements below.

Ice Age	Neanderthals	hunter-gatherers
limited evidence	Bronze Age	Neolithic agricultural revolution
division of labor	anthropologist	artisans
nomads		

1. An _____ is a scientist who studies the remains of skeletons to figure out what early hominids looked like and how long they lived.

2. Artifacts give _____, so scientists must make educated guesses to determine their use.

3. Earth has had several periods of extremely cold weather, known together as the

_____ .

4. Early *Homo sapiens*, called _____, wore animal skins, used fire for warmth and cooking, and buried their dead.

5. The long process known as the _____ marks the important shift from food gathering to food producing.

6. A _____, brought about by improved farming methods, allowed people to specialize in different kinds of work.

7. In a group of _____, men hunt animals and women stay near the campsites to gather plants and fruit.

8. A class of skilled workers, called _____, made products such as tools and traded them for food.

9. The invention of bronze tools marked the end of the Stone Age and the beginning of the _____.

10. _____ were people who wandered from place to place in search of food.

TRUE/FALSE *(2 points each)* Mark each statement *T* if it is true or *F* if it is false.

_____ **1.** Records of cultures and societies could easily be kept without a system of writing.

_____ **2.** One characteristic of a civilization is that the people must be able to produce extra food.

_____ **3.** The development of a calendar and the use of some form of writing are sometimes considered additional characteristics of a civilization.

_____ **4.** The earliest forms of writing used the same letters we use today.

_____ **5.** Iron is easier to make than bronze.

Chapter 1, Chapter Test Form C, continued

IDENTIFICATION *(5 points each)* Determine whether each statement best describes the hunter-gatherer way of life or the agricultural way of life. Write the letter of each statement in the appropriate box.

a. People lived as nomads, moving from place to place in search of food.

b. Fruits and nuts gathered by women and children were a common food source.

c. Animals were domesticated.

d. Crops such as wheat, barley, rice, and millet were grown.

e. Better farming methods allowed for the division of labor.

f. The primary role of men was to hunt for animals.

Hunter-Gatherer Lifestyle	Agricultural Lifestyle
_____	_____
_____	_____
_____	_____

CHAPTER  2

Chapter Test Form C

The First Civilizations

MATCHING *(2 points each)* Place the letters of the descriptions next to the appropriate names and terms.

_____ **1.** barter

_____ **2.** Torah

_____ **3.** mummification

_____ **4.** city-state

_____ **5.** monotheism

_____ **6.** empire

_____ **7.** pharaoh

_____ **8.** hieroglyphics

_____ **9.** polytheism

_____ **10.** Hammurabi

_____ **11.** Abraham

_____ **12.** Hatshepsut

_____ **13.** dynasty

_____ **14.** Phoenician alphabet

_____ **15.** money economy

a. a form of writing developed by the people of the Nile River valley

b. a family of rulers

c. a title used by Egyptian rulers, meaning "great house"

d. believing in many gods

e. a form of government in which a town or city controls the land surrounding it

f. the founder of the Hebrew people, according to the Bible

g. the exchange of one good or service for another

h. Babylonian ruler known for creating a code of law based on the idea of "an eye for an eye"

i. a process of preserving a dead body, in which the organs are removed and the body is treated with chemicals

j. believing in one god

k. economic system that allowed traders to set prices for goods and services

l. one of the first known female rulers, who became a pharaoh of the New Kingdom

m. the first five books of the Old Testament

n. a form of government in which one person, or a single people, rules over many other peoples and their territories

o. a writing system that became the model for later Western alphabets

FILL IN THE BLANK *(3 points each)* Choose from the following list to complete each of the statements below.

Nile River   scribes   Zoroaster
Fertile Crescent   Rosetta Stone   Twelve Tribes of Israel
Sumerians   Great Sphinx

1. Egyptians of the Old Kingdom built the _____, a huge structure with the head of a pharaoh and the body of a lion.

2. According to the Bible, the _____ were formed by the sons of Jacob.

3. The discovery of the _____ enabled scholars to use what they knew about Greek to decode and read hieroglyphics.

4. Teachings of the prophet _____ may have influenced many great religions including Judaism and Christianity.

5. The _____ is one of the most important geographical features of Egypt.

6. The strip of land that arcs through Southwest Asia and is very suitable to farming is called the _____.

7. The _____ lived in the Tigris-Euphrates Valley and may have been the first people to develop and use the wheel.

8. In Egypt, education focused mainly on an elite group of people called _____, or clerks.

TRUE/FALSE *(2 points each)* Mark each statement *T* if it is true or *F* if it is false.

_____ 1. Egyptians lived in an area known as the Fertile Crescent.

_____ 2. Civilizations with strong rulers typically survived longer than those with weak rulers.

_____ 3. Egyptians buried their dead in temples known as ziggurats.

_____ 4. Sumerians considered education important, but educated only upper-class boys.

_____ 5. Over time, many different empires controlled the area known as the Fertile Crescent.

_____ 6. The alphabet we use today is based on the Phoenician alphabet.

_____ 7. The Lydians were the first people to use coined money.

_____ 8. It is believed that Jacob received the Ten Commandments at the top of Mount Sinai.

IDENTIFICATION *(3 points each)* Determine whether each statement best describes the civilizations of Egypt, the Fertile Crescent, or Asia Minor. Write the letter of each statement in the appropriate box.

a. This area was inhabited by the Phoenicians and Lydians.

b. Hieroglyphics were developed by the people of this region.

c. The first settlers here were known as the Sumerians.

d. People of this area gathered shellfish, called murex, to use in making a purple dye.

e. This was the home of the famous Babylonian, Hammurabi, who wrote the Code of Hammurabi.

f. People of this region built pyramids as tombs for their pharaohs.

g. Empires such as the Babylonians, Hittites, Assyrians, and Chaldeans conquered and ruled this area.

h. The first money economy was developed and used here.

i. This area benefited from the natural protection of the deserts and seas surrounding the Nile River.

j. This region developed a form of community called the city-state.

Egypt	Fertile Crescent	Asia Minor

Ancient Indian Civilizations

MATCHING *(3 points each)* Place the letters of the descriptions next to the appropriate names and terms.

_____ **1.** caste system

_____ **2.** Siddhartha Gautama

_____ **3.** reincarnation

_____ **4.** Himalayas

_____ **5.** Panchatantra

_____ **6.** inoculation

_____ **7.** Sanskrit

_____ **8.** nirvana

_____ **9.** Chandra Gupta II

_____ **10.** Indo-Aryans

a. the founder of Buddhism, who became known as Buddha

b. a form of social organization in Indian society

c. the belief that the soul does not die, but is reborn in another form

d. the Indo-Aryan language

e. a place of perfect peace where souls go when the cycle of reincarnation is complete

f. a nomadic people who crossed into northwestern India around 1750 B.C.

g. a mountain range in northern India containing the world's highest peaks

h. the practice of infecting a person with a mild form of a disease in order to prevent the more serious form

i. a set of Indian stories that have been translated into many languages

j. ruler of northern India during what has been called a "golden age"

FILL IN THE BLANK *(3 points each)* Choose from the following list to complete each of the statements below.

Brahmins	Vedas	epics	polygyny
monsoons	raja	Asoka	
Buddhism	Hinduism	suttee	

1. Great works of religious literature, known as the _____, tell us most of what we know about the Indo-Aryans.

2. _____, a practice in which widows throw themselves on top of their husband's flaming funeral pyres, became a common practice in India.

3. _____ was a great leader of the Mauryan dynasty, and later dedicated his life to Buddhist teachings.

4. The "Four Noble Truths" and "The Eightfold Path" are part of

_____.

5. The practice in which men are allowed to have more than one wife is known as

_____.

6. Special priests in the Indo-Aryan society called _____ knew the proper forms and rules for complicated Vedic religious rituals.

7. Strong winds that mark the different seasons in India are called

_____.

8. _____ teaches that certain animals, like cows, are particularly sacred.

9. A _____ ruled each state in the Indo-Aryan society, acting as a military leader, a lawmaker, and a judge.

10. The Bhagavad Gita is one part of the _____, or long poems with historical or religious themes, that were derived from the ideas in the Upanishads.

TRUE/FALSE *(2 points each)* Mark each statement *T* if it is true or *F* if it is false.

_____ **1.** Asoka ruled the Mauryan Empire as part of the Gupta dynasty.

_____ **2.** The early years of the Gupta dynasty have been called a "golden age" of India.

_____ **3.** The Mauryans became the first imperial dynasty to hold nearly all of India.

_____ **4.** The Mauryan dynasty was disorganized and lacked a centralized government.

_____ **5.** The Guptas favored Hinduism, but they also supported Buddhism.

Chapter 3, Chapter Test Form C, continued

IDENTIFICATION *(5 points each)* Complete the diagram about Hinduism and Buddhism by writing the letter of each item in the appropriate place.

   a. two important principles are dharma and kharma

   b. believe in reincarnation

   c. believe any person, regardless of caste, can reach nirvana

   d. most famous scripture is known as the Bhagavad Gita

   e. spread along major trade routes

   f. founded by Siddhartha Gautama

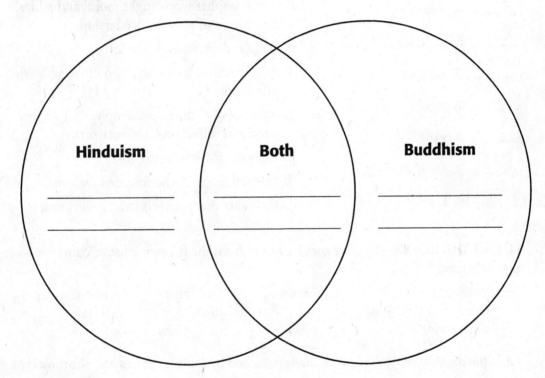

Chapter Test Form C
Ancient Chinese Civilization

MATCHING *(3 points each)* Place the letters of the descriptions next to the appropriate terms.

_____ 1. loess

_____ 2. animism

_____ 3. bureaucracy

_____ 4. autocracy

_____ 5. genealogy

_____ 6. Legalism

_____ 7. yin

_____ 8. yang

_____ 9. Confucious

_____ 10. Laozi

a. a record of a family tree

b. a system of government in which an emperor has complete power

c. fertile, yellow soil found in the Huang River

d. a philosopher who taught moral and ethical behavior and virtuous leadership

e. female, dark, and passive force

f. a government organized into different levels and tasks

g. a school of Chinese philosophy that viewed people as selfish and untrustworthy

h. male, bright, and active force

i. the philosopher who founded Daoism

j. the belief that spirits inhabit everything

FILL IN THE BLANK *(3 points each)* Choose from the following list to complete each of the statements below.

leveling	animism	Buddhism	Five Classics
Great Wall of China	Xia	dikes	
civil service	*Analects*	calligraphy	

1. One dynasty controlled price changes caused by food surpluses and shortages using

   a system called _____.

2. Different sections of the _____ were built by many dynasties to keep invaders out of China.

3. The _____ system remained an important part of Chinese government until the early 1900s A.D.

4. _____ built by early farmers to protect their crops from flooding eventually caused the Huang River to rise well above the surrounding land.

5. During the Shang period, a religion was developed that combined

   _____ and ancestor worship.

6. A line of kings, called the _____, ruled the Huang River region starting about 2200 B.C.

7. During the Han dynasty, missionaries from India brought the teachings of

_____ into China.

8. _____ is an art form that developed from a form of writing.

9. The teachings of Confucius were collected into a work called the

_____.

10. Civil servants in ancient China studied a set of texts known as the

_____.

TRUE/FALSE *(2 points each)* Mark each statement *T* if it is true or *F* if it is false.

_____ **1.** The school of Chinese philosophy called Legalism had more influence on Chinese life than any other philosophy.

_____ **2.** The Huang River was called "China's Sorrow" because it often flooded and destroyed crops.

_____ **3.** The Han were probably the first to introduce flood control and irrigation systems into China.

_____ **4.** The Shang Dynasty was China's first historic dynasty.

_____ **5.** The family is the most important factor in Chinese society.

Chapter 4, Chapter Test Form C, continued

IDENTIFICATION *(3 points each)* Determine which word or phrase describes each of the main dynasties of China. Write the letter of each statement in the appropriate box.

a. Silk Road

b. no central government

c. lasted the longest

d. Cheng (Shih Huang Ti)

e. autocracy

f. Liu Ch'e (Wu Ti)

g. civil service system

h. creative period for Chinese philosophy

i. lasted only 15 years

j. leveling

Zhou Dynasty	Qin Dynasty	Han Dynasty
_____	_____	_____
_____	_____	_____
_____	_____	_____
		_____

 **UNIT 1**

Unit Test Form C

The Beginnings of Civilization

MATCHING *(3 points each)* Place the letters of the descriptions next to the appropriate names.

_____ **1.** Abraham

_____ **2.** Hatshepsut

_____ **3.** Confucious

_____ **4.** Laozi

_____ **5.** Lucy

_____ **6.** Donald Johanson

_____ **7.** Siddhartha Gautama

_____ **8.** Asoka

_____ **9.** Chandra Gupta II

_____ **10.** Cheng (Shih Huang Ti)

a. ruler of the Qin dynasty, whose name means "first emperor"

b. the name given to a 3 million-year-old female hominid skeleton

c. the founder of the Hebrew people, according to the Bible

d. philosopher who founded Daoism

e. the founder of Buddhism

f. an anthropologist who discovered a hominid skeleton in Ethiopia

g. one of the first known female rulers, who was a pharaoh in the New Kingdon

h. an Indian ruler and devout Buddhist who sent missionaries to other regions

i. a Chinese philosopher whose collected teachings and ideas are called the *Analects*

j. a ruler of northern India during what was called a "golden age"

FILL IN THE BLANK *(3 points each)* Choose from the following list to complete each of the statements below.

civilization   animism   inoculation
reincarnation   cultural diffusion polytheism
caste system   artifacts   money economy
barter

1. _____ is the belief that spirits inhabit everything.

2. The exchange of one good or service for another is called

_____.

3. _____ are objects, such as tools, clothing, works of art, weapons, and toys, that were made and used by early hominids.

4. Many Egyptians held a belief called _____, meaning they believed in the existence of many different gods.

5. In a _____, people use money as a measure of value and a unit of account.

6. A _____ has at least these three characteristics: the ability to produce extra food; large cities or towns with some form of government; and people within a community performing different jobs.

7. The _____ was a complicated form of social classes that appeared in India.

8. The spread of ideas and other aspects of culture from one area to another is known

   as _____.

9. _____ is the belief that after death, one's soul will be reborn in another form.

10. _____ is a medical technique in which a person is infected with a mild form of a disease in order to prevent the more serious form.

TRUE/FALSE *(2 points each)* Mark each statement *T* if it is true or *F* if it is false.

_____ **1.** Mummification was practiced by the Egyptians.

_____ **2.** Artifacts provide a great deal of information, making it easy for scientists to determine how they were used.

_____ **3.** Over time, the Fertile Crescent was ruled by many different civilizations.

_____ **4.** One ancient Chinese philosophy believes that everything in the world results from the balance between the yin and the yang.

_____ **5.** Daoism was a religion practiced by the Sumerians.

Unit 1, Unit Test Form C, continued

IDENTIFICATION *(3 points each)* Fill in the chart below by determining which culture is associated with each of these beliefs or characteristics. Write the letter of each description in the appropriate box.

a. created the caste system

b. believed in yin and yang

c. wrote using hieroglyphics

d. beginnings of Buddhism and Hinduism

e. ruled by pharaohs

f. began economic policy of leveling

g. enjoyed the stories of the Panchatantra, a collection of fables

h. developed Confucianism and Daoism

i. built pyramids and the Great Sphinx

j. family was the most important factor in society

Egyptian Culture	Indian Culture	Chinese Culture
_____	_____	_____
_____	_____	_____
_____	_____	_____
		_____

CHAPTER  **5**   Chapter Test Form C

The Greek City-States

MATCHING *(3 points each)* Place the letters of the descriptions next to the appropriate terms.

_____ **1.** acropolis

_____ **2.** epic

_____ **3.** ephors

_____ **4.** polis

_____ **5.** import

_____ **6.** export

_____ **7.** terracing

_____ **8.** myth

_____ **9.** oracle

_____ **10.** metics

a. traditional story about gods, goddesses, or heroes

b. a group in Athenian society made up of people born outside of Athens

c. five people elected to make sure the Spartan kings stayed within the law

d. a hill where most public buildings in a city-state were built

e. a good or service sold to another country or region

f. a long poem about heroes or great events

g. a place where Greeks believed that the gods spoke through priests or priestesses

h. the Greek word for city-state

i. a method of farming where small, flat plots of land are carved into the hillside

j. a good or service brought in from another country or region

FILL IN THE BLANK *(3 points each)* Choose from the following list to complete each of the statements below.

archons   agora   Battle of Marathon
popular government   Minoan   direct democracy
Battle of Thermopylae   aristocracies   representative democracy
pedagogue

1. The main public meeting place in each polis was the _____, or marketplace.

2. The _____ civilization was the earliest Greek civilization.

3. Greek city-states that were governed by groups of noblemen were known as

_____.

4. _____ is based on the idea that people can and should rule themselves.

Chapter 5, Chapter Test Form C, continued

5. Citizens elect people to govern for them in a _____.

6. In a _____, all citizens directly participate in making decisions.

7. In Athens, a _____ taught manners to young boys.

8. Athenian citizens elected nine _____, who each served as ruler for one year.

9. Athenians defeated the Persians at the _____.

10. Spartans were defeated by the Persians at the _____.

TRUE/FALSE *(2 points each)* Mark each statement *T* if it is true or *F* if it is false.

_____ **1.** Greece has many long rivers, which made travel between villages easy.

_____ **2.** During the Homeric Age, Greeks relied on religion to explain natural events such as the change of seasons.

_____ **3.** Athenian society included three main social groups: equals, half-citizens, and helots.

_____ **4.** Sophists created schools to teach Athenian boys how to fight.

_____ **5.** Athens controlled an alliance of Greek city-states called the Delian League.

Chapter 5, Chapter Test Form C, continued

IDENTIFICATION *(3 points each)* Determine which term best describes each of the following city-states. Write the letter of each statement in the appropriate box.

a. ephors

b. acropolis

c. sea traders

d. half-citizens

e. military society

f. Draco

g. equals

h. valley

i. Sophists

j. metics

Sparta	Athens
_____	_____
_____	_____
_____	_____
_____	_____
_____	_____

Name _____ Class _____ Date _____

Chapter Test Form C

Greece's Golden and Hellenistic Ages

MATCHING *(3 points each)* Place the letters of the descriptions next to the appropriate names.

_____ **1.** Myron

_____ **2.** Plato

_____ **3.** Sophocles

_____ **4.** Hippocrates

_____ **5.** Aristophanes

_____ **6.** Zeno

_____ **7.** Archimedes

_____ **8.** Aristarchus

_____ **9.** Eratosthenes

_____ **10.** Phidias

_____ **11.** Socrates

_____ **12.** Aristotle

_____ **13.** Euclid

_____ **14.** Phidias

_____ **15.** Herodotus

a. playwright; wrote *Oedipus Rex*

b. scientist; calculated the value of pi

c. astronomer; calculated the distance around Earth

d. sculptor; created the Parthenon's statue of Athena

e. philosopher; was executed for his beliefs

f. sculptor; sculpted *The Discus Thrower*

g. mathematician; best known for work in the field of geometry

h. established the Stoic philosophy in Athens

i. playwright; wrote *The Trojan Women*

j. astronomer; believed Earth moved around the sun

k. philosopher; founded the Academy, a school for teaching philosophy

l. great writer of Greek comedies

m. considered the founder of modern medicine

n. philosopher; books included *Ethics* and *Poetics*

o. first historian of the Western world

FILL IN THE BLANK *(3 points each)* Choose from the following list to complete each of the statements below.

orator   aristocracy   philosophy
phalanxes   dramas

1. Demosthenes led Athenian opposition to Philip II of Macedon using his skills as a

great _____, or public speaker.

2. The development of _____, or the study of questions of reality and human existence, was one of the Greek's greatest achievements.

3. A government ruled by an upper class is called an _____.

Chapter 6, Chapter Test Form C, continued

4. The Greeks were the first people to write _____, or plays containing action or dialogue.

5. Philip II of Macedon used the Greek idea of organizing an army into

_____, or rows of soldiers standing shoulder to shoulder.

TRUE/FALSE *(2 points each)* Mark each statement *T* if it is true or *F* if it is false.

_____ **1.** The Parthenon was an important temple built to honor Zeus.

_____ **2.** Philip II of Macedon and Alexander the Great both died in battle.

_____ **3.** Art was important to the Greeks because it was a major source of income.

_____ **4.** Philip II conquered and united Greece.

_____ **5.** Alexandria, Egypt, was a leading trade center and the biggest Hellenistic city.

_____ **6.** The main character in Greek tragedies was often punished for having too much pride.

_____ **7.** Philip II was the son of Alexander the Great.

_____ **8.** Women were given more rights during Hellenistic times.

_____ **9.** The Parthenon was built on the Acropolis in Athens.

_____ **10.** After Alexander the Great died, his empire was divided into four main kingdoms—Greece, Macedon, Egypt, and Syria.

Chapter 6, Chapter Test Form C, continued

IDENTIFICATION *(3 points each)* Identify which of the following events occurred before Philip II conquered Greece, and which events occurred after. Write the letter of each statement in the appropriate box.

a. Alexander the Great expands the Greek Empire.

b. The Parthenon is built.

c. Four schools of philosophy—Cynicism, Skepticism, Stoicism, and Epicureanism—influence Greek thought.

d. Greece enters the golden age.

e. The Archimedes screw is invented.

f. Hippocrates writes 60 to 70 medical studies.

g. The Greek Empire is divided into three kingdoms.

h. Socrates teaches that education is the key to personal growth.

i. Greek artists begin making lifelike sculptures.

j. Education becomes more widespread.

Philip II of Macedon Conquers Greece in 333 B.C.

Before	After
_____	_____
_____	_____
_____	_____
_____	_____
_____	_____

CHAPTER  7

Chapter Test Form C

The Roman World

MATCHING *(2 points each)* Place the letters of the descriptions next to the appropriate names and terms.

_____ **1.** Hannibal

_____ **2.** the Gracchi

_____ **3.** Gnaeus Pompey

_____ **4.** Attila

_____ **5.** Jesus

_____ **6.** Virgil

_____ **7.** Ptolemy

_____ **8.** plebeians

_____ **9.** Cleopatra

_____ **10.** Augustus Caesar

_____ **11.** Vandals

_____ **12.** Julius Caesar

_____ **13.** Spartacus

_____ **14.** Constantine

_____ **15.** Julio-Claudian Emperors

a. Roman emperor who created the new capital city in the East called Constantinople

b. German invaders whose name has come to mean "one who destroys another's property"

c. largest class of people in the early Roman Republic, made up of farmers and workers

d. popular Roman general who served as part of Caesar's First Triumvirate

e. leader of the Huns

f. astronomer who believed the sun, the planets, and the stars revolved around Earth

g. great Spanish general who fought many battles against Rome in the Second Punic War

h. name given to the relatives of Julius Caesar who ruled the Roman empire

i. Roman slave who led a revolt to gain freedom

j. daughter of the ruling family in Egypt whom Caesar put in power as a Roman ally

k. Jewish teacher whose followers founded Christianity

l. two brothers who tried to reform the weakening Roman Republic

m. considered the greatest Roman poet

n. powerful Roman leader who was killed by conspirators in the Senate

o. grandnephew and heir of Julius Caesar, also known as Octavian

FILL IN THE BLANK *(3 points each)* Choose from the following list to complete each of the statements below.

pope	veto	martyrs
aqueducts	gladiators	inflation
rabbis	censors	checks and balances
dictator		

Chapter 7, Chapter Test Form C, continued

1. A consul could _____, or refuse to approve, the acts of other consuls.

2. A citizen who is named absolute ruler is also called a _____.

3. The Romans built _____ to carry water from the mountains.

4. _____ were trained fighters, usually slaves, who entertained large crowds.

5. Christians who were put to death because of their religious beliefs were called

_____.

6. The _____ is the patriarch of Rome, and claims to be supreme over all other patriarchs.

7. A rise in prices caused by a decrease in the value of money is called

_____.

8. _____, or Jewish scholars who interpret scripture, led Jewish congregations after the Romans destroyed the Second Temple at Jerusalem.

9. The principle of _____ prevents any one part of the government from becoming too powerful.

10. _____ registered citizens according to their wealth, appointed candidates to the Senate and oversaw the moral conduct of all citizens.

TRUE/FALSE (2 points each) Mark each statement T if it is true or F if it is false.

_____ 1. The United States uses some of the same principles of government that were established by the Romans.

_____ 2. Some of the roads built by Romans still exist today.

_____ 3. The wealthy people of Rome lived a simple life without many luxuries.

_____ 4. Historians can point to one single event that caused the fall of the Roman empire.

_____ 5. Roman influence is still evident throughout the world.

Chapter 7, Chapter Test Form C, continued

ORGANIZATION *(5 points each)* Complete the flowchart to show the order in which the following events happened. Write the letter of each statement in the appropriate box.

 a. Julius Caesar comes to power.

 b. The Roman Empire falls.

 c. The Second Triumvirate, with Augustus Caesar, takes control.

 d. The Roman Republic is founded.

 e. Julius Caesar is killed in the Senate.

 f. Rome fights in the Punic Wars.

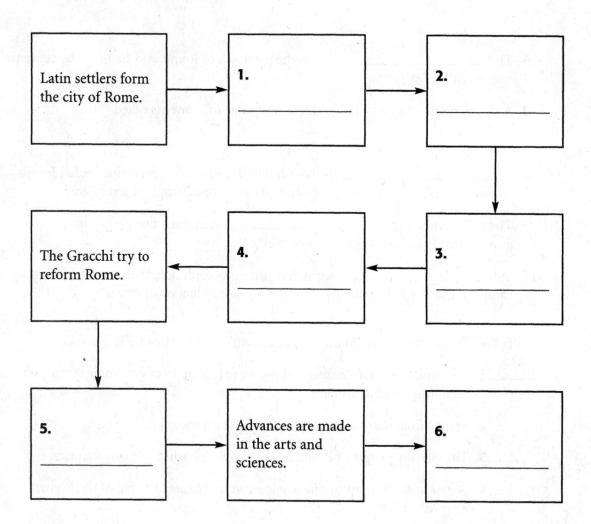

CHAPTER **8**

Chapter Test Form C

Africa

MATCHING *(3 points each)* Place the letters of the descriptions next to the appropriate terms.

_____ **1.** tropical rain forest

_____ **2.** Swahili

_____ **3.** gold-for-salt exchange

_____ **4.** matrilineal

_____ **5.** Bantu

_____ **6.** savannas

_____ **7.** griots

_____ **8.** jungle

_____ **9.** oral traditions

_____ **10.** linguist

a. vast stretches of grassland found in Africa

b. highly trained speakers and entertainers who memorized the oral traditions of their village

c. ancestors and inherited property are traced through the mother rather than the father

d. vast forests that receive more than 100 inches of rain each year

e. important trade agreement between cities in Africa and Europe

f. Bantu language with Arabic and Persian influences

g. areas of the rainforest where dense tangles of plants grow

h. poems, songs, and stories passed by word of mouth from one generation to another

i. a scientist who studies languages

j. a family of closely related African languages that spread throughout the continent

FILL IN THE BLANK *(3 points each)* Choose from the following list to complete each of the statements below.

Mount Kilimanjaro	Sahara Desert	Great Zimbabwe	Sonni ʻAlī
Tunka Manin	Shona	Great Rift Valley	
Mansa Mūsā	King ʻEzānā	Mohammed I Askia	

1. The _____ was formed millions of years ago when the Earth's crust parted.

2. One of the most powerful Ghanian rulers was _____.

3. _____, a rebel leader, captured Timbuktu and built up the kingdom of Songhai.

4. Sonni ʻAlī's successor, _____, made Timbuktu a great commercial center.

5. The enormous _____ covers about one-fourth of the African continent.

6. _____ of Aksum converted to Christianity during his reign, making it a powerful influence in the region.

7. The great ruler of Mali, _____, reigned in the early 1300s.

8. _____ was the greatest of the fortresses built by the Shona.

9. The _____ were a people that migrated onto the plateau of what is today Zimbabwe.

10. _____ is a dormant volcano on the eastern part of the African plateau.

TRUE/FALSE *(2 points each)* Mark each statement *T* if it is true or *F* if it is false.

_____ **1.** The climate of Africa is the same throughout the continent.

_____ **2.** Trade was not an important part of the economy of West Africa.

_____ **3.** Scientists have found evidence that the people of Africa exchanged ideas and knowledge with parts of Asia.

_____ **4.** Historians believe that some societies in Africa traced their ancestors and inherited property through their mothers, rather than their fathers.

_____ **5.** Christianity became a powerful influence in eastern Africa.

Chapter 8, Chapter Test Form C, continued

IDENTIFICATION *(5 points each)* Fill in the chart below by matching each problem with its solution. Write the letter of the problem to the left of the arrow, and the letter of the solution to the right.

a. Farmers grew root crops.

b. Dry grasslands made farming wheat and barley difficult.

c. The gold-for-salt exchange was established.

d. Jungles in the rainforest let in little sunlight for growing plants.

e. People of the Sahel mined gold, but needed salt to flavor and preserve their food.

f. Farmers domesticated different grains like millet and sorghum.

Problem	Solution
1. _____ →	2. _____
3. _____ →	4. _____
5. _____ →	6. _____

CHAPTER  9

Chapter Test Form C
The Americas

MATCHING (*3 points each*) Place the letters of the descriptions next to the appropriate terms.

_____ **1.** Beringia

_____ **2.** totem poles

_____ **3.** potlatches

_____ **4.** adobe

_____ **5.** tepees

_____ **6.** strait

_____ **7.** chinampas

_____ **8.** quipu

_____ **9.** buffalo

_____ **10.** Quechua

a. animal hunted by the people of the Great Plains

b. a method of keeping records by making a series of knots on parallel strings

c. the land bridge used by the people of Asia to move into the Americas

d. festive gatherings in which a clan's leader would display the clan's material goods and then give them away to guests

e. cone-shaped tents made from animal hides

f. sun-dried brick used to build houses

g. great wooden carvings of people and beasts that represent a community's history

h. was once the official language of the Inca

i. raised fields made with mud taken from the bottom of lakes

j. a narrow strip of water separating two land masses

FILL IN THE BLANK (*3 points each*) Choose from the following list to complete each of the statements below.

Pueblo	Cahokia	Inca
Mississippians	Maya	Quetzalcoatl
Hohokam	Aztecs	Olmec
Toltec		

1. _____ was a Toltec god, represented by a feathered serpent.

2. The _____ settled on the island of Lake Texcoco and built a city called Tenochtitlán.

3. The _____ lived in what is today the southwestern United States, near present-day Arizona.

4. The _____ were a group of people that lived in the Eastern Woodlands region near the Mississippi River.

Chapter 9, Chapter Test Form C, continued

5. The _____ raised corn and built houses with adobe.

6. The city of _____ was located near present-day East St. Louis, and was the largest ceremonial center of North America.

7. The name _____ means "children of the sun."

8. The _____ were considered the most advanced people of the Americas.

9. The earliest culture to be established in Central America is believed to be the

    _____ civilization.

10. The _____ people named their capital city Tula.

TRUE/FALSE *(2 points each)* Mark each statement *T* if it is true or *F* if it is false.

_____ 1. Inca surgeons could perform operations on the brain.

_____ 2. People of the Eastern Woodlands built mounds in the shapes of animals.

_____ 3. Aztecs did not believe in human sacrifice.

_____ 4. Almost every type of climate and terrain can be found somewhere in the Americas.

_____ 5. The Maya developed the only complete writing system constructed by an early culture in the Americas.

Chapter 9, Chapter Test Form C, continued

IDENTIFICATION *(5 points each)* Complete the chart by filling in the letter of the correct phrase. Choose your answers from the list below.

   a. worshipped the Sun god

   b. built tepees from animal skins

   c. held ceremonies before and after hunts

   d. farmed on chinampas

   e. built cities with pyramid-temples, marketplaces, and palaces

   f. hunted for buffalo

	Great Plains	**Aztec**
Sources of Food	_____	_____
Buildings	_____	_____
Religious Practices	_____	_____

UNIT 2

Unit Test Form C

The Growth of Civilizations

MATCHING *(2 points each)* Place the letters of the descriptions next to the appropriate names.

_____ **1.** Plato

_____ **2.** Socrates

_____ **3.** Aristotle

_____ **4.** Archimedes

_____ **5.** Jesus

_____ **6.** Julius Caesar

_____ **7.** Constantine

_____ **8.** Mansa Mūsā

_____ **9.** Inca

_____ **10.** Quetzalcoatl

_____ **11.** Pueblo

_____ **12.** Maya

_____ **13.** Aztec

_____ **14.** Hippocrates

_____ **15.** Spartacus

a. famous ruler of Ghana, who made a pilgrimage to Mecca

b. philosopher who used a method of teaching through questioning

c. kept records using a series of knots on parallel strings, known as quipu

d. considered to be the founder of modern medicine

e. Jewish teacher who was crucified and, according to the Gospels, arose from the dead

f. Roman slave who led a revolt for freedom

g. philosopher who wrote *The Republic*

h. created a capital city in the eastern part of the Roman empire

i. people of southwestern North America who built with adobe bricks

j. student of Plato, known for his skill in defining and classifying things

k. wandering warriors who settled and built the city of Tenochtitlán

l. god of the Toltec people, represented by a feathered serpent

m. considered the most advanced people of the Americas

n. calculated the value of pi (π)

o. popular Roman leader who was killed by members of the Senate

FILL IN THE BLANK *(3 points each)* Choose from the following list to complete each of the statements below.

Minoan	Beringia	Philip II of Macedon
oracles	terracing	gold-for-salt exchange
checks and balances	democracy	Julio-Claudian Emperors
Quechua		

1. _____ was known for his well-disciplined army, which he organized into phalanxes.

2. A method of farming, known as _____, carves small, flat plots into the sides of hills.

3. A trade agreement between the kingdoms of West Africa and Europe was called the

   _____.

4. A system of _____ prevents any one part of the government from gaining too much power.

5. The earliest Greek civilization was known as the _____ civilization.

6. The _____ were relatives of Julius Caesar who ruled Rome after his death.

7. Greeks would often travel to _____ to ask questions about the future.

8. _____ was once the official language of the Inca empire.

9. A government that is ruled by the people or elected representatives of the people is

   called a _____.

10. _____ is the name of the area around the land bridge that once connected Asia and North America.

TRUE/FALSE (2 points each) Mark each statement *T* if it is true or *F* if it is false.

_____ 1. A devastating plague killed many Athenians, including the great leader Pericles.

_____ 2. Plato is considered the most powerful of the kings of Macedon.

_____ 3. Julius Caesar was part of the First Triumvirate.

_____ 4. Trade was an important contributor to the rise of many African civilizations.

_____ 5. Cultures in the Americas differed greatly, depending on where people settled.

Unit 2, Unit Test Form C, continued

IDENTIFICATION *(5 points each)* Fill in the chart below by matching each geographical feature with the correct region. Write the letter of each description on the appropriate line.

a. land stretches more than 9,000 miles from the north to the south

b. terrain includes rain forests, huge deserts, and the Great Rift Valley

c. the sea played an important role in the lives of the people of this region

d. two of the world's longest rivers—the Mississippi River and the Amazon River—are found here

e. short mountain ranges cut up the mainland, separating the villages

f. home to Mount Kilimanjaro

Greece	Africa	The Americas
_____	_____	_____
_____	_____	_____

CHAPTER 10

Modern Chapter 1

Chapter Test Form C

The Byzantine Empire and Russia

MATCHING *(3 points each)* Place the letters of the descriptions next to the appropriate terms.

_____ **1.** czar

_____ **2.** excommunication

_____ **3.** mosaic

_____ **4.** icon

_____ **5.** *oprichniki*

_____ **6.** steppe

_____ **7.** boyars

_____ **8.** dowry

_____ **9.** taiga

_____ **10.** heresy

a. a holy picture of Jesus, the Virgin Mary, or the saints

b. grassy, treeless land with black, fertile soil

c. geographical region that has great forests and receives much rainfall

d. money or goods a wife brings to a husband at marriage

e. an opinion that conflicts with official church beliefs

f. councils made up of nobles, who gave advice to the ruling princes

g. iconoclasts were threatened with this, meaning they could not be members of the church anymore

h. a picture or design made from small pieces of enamel, glass, or stone

i. personal group of civil servants formed by "Ivan the Terrible"

j. title meaning "caesar," taken by Ivan IV

FILL IN THE BLANK *(3 points each)* Choose from the following list to complete each of the statements below.

Justinian Code	Slavs	Iconoclastic Controversy
third Rome	Hagia Sophia	Ottoman Turks
Greek fire	Methodius	Pravda Russkia
Vladimir I		

1. The word "slave" comes from the frequent servitude of the people known as

_____ .

2. _____ and his brother Cyril were Christian missionaries who created the Cyrillic alphabet to teach the Bible in central and eastern Europe.

3. The _____ , meaning "holy wisdom," is an example of the great religious architecture created by the Byzantines.

4. Russia's first law code, known as _____, was introduced by Yaroslov the Wise.

5. Chemical weapons known as "_____" were used on ships in the Byzantine navy.

6. The _____ was the debate between opponents and defenders of religious icons.

7. The Byzantine Empire was threatened by a rising Asian power known as the

_____.

8. _____ converted to Christianity, and ordered all Kievans to become Christians.

9. Russians proclaimed Moscow to be the "_____."

10. The laws of the Roman Empire were compiled in a four-part collection known as the

_____.

TRUE/FALSE *(2 points each)* Mark each statement *T* if it is true or *F* if it is false.

_____ **1.** The Christian Church was an important part of life in the Byzantine Empire.

_____ **2.** Trade was difficult in Russia because there were few rivers to use for transportation.

_____ **3.** Russians used town meetings as a way for free men to discuss concerns and express opinions.

_____ **4.** "Ivan the Terrible" was also known for his important contributions to the Russian state.

_____ **5.** Russians built beautiful churches to inspire awe, religious wonder, and mystical feelings of spirituality among people.

Chapter 10, Chapter Test Form C, continued

IDENTIFICATION *(5 points each)* Fill in the chart by determining which beliefs are those of the Roman Catholic Church, and which are beliefs of the Eastern Orthodox Church. Place the letter of the correct description into its proper category below.

- **a.** rejected the honoring of icons, then later accepted it
- **b.** did not allow married priests
- **c.** believed the Roman pope was the supreme leader of the church
- **d.** accepted the honoring of icons
- **e.** allowed priests to be married
- **f.** believed the local leaders ruled the church

Roman Catholic Church	Eastern Orthodox Church
_____	_____
_____	_____
_____	_____

CHAPTER  Chapter Test Form C

Modern Chapter 2   **The Islamic World**

MATCHING *(3 points each)* Place the letters of the descriptions next to the appropriate terms.

_____ 1. minaret

_____ 2. imams

_____ 3. sultan

_____ 4. astrolabe

_____ 5. Muslims

_____ 6. sheikh

_____ 7. caliph

_____ 8. bedouins

_____ 9. Muhammad

_____ 10. jihad

a. followers of Islam

b. nomadic herders of sheep and camels on the Arabian Peninsula

c. title given to Abū Bakr, meaning "successor to the Prophet"

d. descendants of 'Alī, whom the Shi'ah believe should decide religious and worldly matters

e. the founder of Islam

f. title given to the ruler of the Turks

g. small instrument that allowed observers to chart the positions of the stars and thus calculate their own position on Earth

h. a tower attached to the outside of a mosque

i. an important part of Islam, meaning "the struggle to defend the faith"

j. a leader of a bedouin tribe

FILL IN THE BLANK *(3 points each)* Choose from the following list to complete each of the statements below.

Tariq	Kaaba	Islam
al-Rāzī	mosques	*The Thousand and One Nights*
Qur'an	hijrah	Five Pillars of Islam
Moors		

1. _____ are Muslim places of worship.

2. Muhammad converted many of the bedouin tribes to _____.

3. The five basic acts of worship required of all Muslims are called the

_____.

4. The holy book of Islam is called the _____.

5. The _____ is a stone building in Mecca that serves as a spiritual sanctuary for Muslims.

6. The journey made by Muhammad from Mecca to Yathrib is called the

   _____, meaning "flight" or "migration."

7. A Berber general named _____ led a Muslim army to conquer Spain.

8. _____ was one of the greatest doctors of the Islamic world.

9. Muslims who made their home in Spain were known as

   _____.

10. A collection of stories called _____ includes the tales of "Sinbad the Sailor," "Aladdin," and "Ali Baba and the Forty Thieves."

TRUE/FALSE *(2 points each)* Mark each statement *T* if it is true or *F* if it is false.

_____ 1. Muhammad was born into a wealthy family and received a formal education.

_____ 2. Muslims worship in mosques filled with religious pictures.

_____ 3. Muslims allowed Christians and Jews whom they conquered to choose either to accept Islam or to pay extra taxes.

_____ 4. The Moors unsuccessfully attempted to invade and control France.

_____ 5. Trade made the Islamic Empire wealthy.

Chapter 11, Chapter Test Form C, continued

IDENTIFICATION *(5 points each)* Place the following events into the order in which they occurred. Write the letter of each description in the correct sequence on the following lines.

_____ 1.

_____ 2.

_____ 3.

_____ 4.

_____ 5.

_____ 6.

a. A Berber general leads a Muslim army to conquer Spain.

b. Muhammad is born.

c. Ibn-Sīnā writes a medical textbook called *Canon of Medicine*.

d. Abū Bakr becomes the caliph.

e. The religion of Islam is founded.

f. The Islamic community divides into two groups, called the Sunni and the Shi'ah.

Modern Chapter **3**

Chapter Test Form C

The Civilizations of East Asia

MATCHING *(3 points each)* Place the letters of the descriptions next to the appropriate names.

_____ **1.** Genghis Khan

_____ **2.** Marco Polo

_____ **3.** Bushido

_____ **4.** Kublai Khan

_____ **5.** Li Bo

_____ **6.** Yi dynasty

_____ **7.** Xi'an

_____ **8.** Zen

_____ **9.** Empress Wu

_____ **10.** Fujiwara

a. capital city of the Tang dynasty, with about 2 million residents

b. Mongol leader who conquered Tibet, but failed to take Japan

c. Italian merchant and explorer who befriended Kublai Khan

d. Daoist poet known for his love of life

e. Tang leader, and the only woman to hold the Chinese throne in her own name

f. fiercest Mongol leader, whose name means "Universal Ruler"

g. ruling dynasty of Korea after the Mongols were driven out in 1392

h. family who first gained control over Japan's central government

i. the most famous sect of Buddhism in Japan

j. the code of behavior followed by the samurai

FILL IN THE BLANK *(3 points each)* Choose from the following list to complete each of the statements below.

samurai	Du Fu	tea ceremony
footbinding	*Diamond Sutra*	Golden Horde
The Tale of Genji	kamikaze	Grand Canal
shogun		

1. The custom of _____ spread among the wealthy Chinese, leaving many women crippled.

2. Europeans called the Mongolian invaders the _____, because of the way their tents looked in the sun.

3. The name _____, meaning "Divine Wind," was given to the typhoon that wrecked a Mongol fleet invading Japan.

4. The world's first known printed book was the _____.

Chapter 12, Chapter Test Form C, continued

5. The Japanese _____ is an art form designed to produce spiritual calm and appreciate the beauty of nature.

6. _____, the world's first novel, was written by Murasaki Shikibu.

7. In feudal Japan, the _____ had control of the military, finances, and laws.

8. The _____ is the world's oldest and longest system of connected waterways.

9. The poet _____ wrote about social issues such as the ongoing frontier wars and destructive uprisings in Tang China.

10. Hired warriors, known as _____, were similar to European knights because of their loyalty to their lord and their skill with a sword.

TRUE/FALSE *(2 points each)* Mark each statement *T* if it is true or *F* if it is false.

_____ **1.** Gunpowder and printing were invented by the Japanese.

_____ **2.** Porcelain, a fine china, was a valuable trade export for the Chinese.

_____ **3.** The Mongols' strong military made it possible to achieve many conquests and gain much territory.

_____ **4.** The main religion in Japan was Christianity.

_____ **5.** The terrain of Korean is mostly grasslands and desert.

Chapter 12, Chapter Test Form C, continued

IDENTIFICATION *(5 points each)* Decide whether each of the following statements about the Sung dynasty are true or false. Write the letter of each phrase in the correct box.

a. The civil service system was eliminated.

b. More Chinese than ever before lived in towns and cities.

c. Tea became an important crop for farmers.

d. Poverty was ignored by the government.

e. Taxation was at very low levels.

f. Foreign trade expanded.

True	False
_____	_____
_____	_____
_____	_____

CHAPTER  13

Chapter Test Form C

Modern Chapter **4**

The Rise of the Middle Ages

MATCHING *(2 points each)* Place the letters of the descriptions next to the appropriate terms.

_____ **1.** tithe

_____ **2.** heretics

_____ **3.** feudalism

_____ **4.** fief

_____ **5.** simony

_____ **6.** abbot

_____ **7.** sacraments

_____ **8.** vassal

_____ **9.** medieval

_____ **10.** interdict

_____ **11.** chivalry

_____ **12.** serfs

_____ **13.** primogeniture

_____ **14.** shires

_____ **15.** canon law

a. Middle Ages; a time of transition

b. system of government that created power for small, independent leaders, often local lords

c. land granted by a local lord

d. system of inheritance that became common in feudalism

e. person who receives a land grant from a lord

f. governmental districts created by the Anglo-Saxons

g. a practice allowing people to buy high positions within the church hierarchy

h. monk who was elected head of his community

i. code of law used by the Catholic Church

j. a tax on a Christian's income, collected by the Catholic Church

k. a ruling by the Catholic Church against an entire region; often used to influence politics

l. Catholic Church ceremonies designed to gain favor with God

m. peasant workers, who had few rights

n. people accused of denying the truth of the Catholic Church's principles

o. system of rules that dictated knights' behavior toward others

FILL IN THE BLANK *(3 points each)* Choose from the following list to complete each of the statements below.

Charlemagne   Magna Carta   Saint Patrick
monasticism   Innocent III   Vikings
Gregory VII   Inquisition   Thomas Becket
Saint Benedict

1. The way of life practiced by nuns and monks was known as

_____ .

2. _____ was a missionary known for bringing Christianity to Ireland.

3. The brutal movement known as the _____ was ordered by the Catholic Church to find people who opposed church doctrines.

4. The Archbishop of Canterbury, _____, opposed attempts to try clergy in royal courts.

5. The _____ influenced both the British and the United States constitutions.

6. _____ did much to strengthen the power of the church, and was known as the strongest of the medieval popes.

7. Declared by the pope to be "Emperor of the Romans," _____ united most of the Christian lands in Western Europe.

8. The _____ often looted and raided settlements that they encountered, taking the people that lived there as slaves.

9. _____ wrote rules to govern monks' lives that were later followed by monks and nuns all over Europe.

10. _____ excommunicated Henry IV, beginning a conflict between church and state that lasted throughout the Middle Ages.

TRUE/FALSE (2 points each) Mark each statement T if it is true or F if it is false.

_____ 1. Italy and Germany were united throughout the Middle Ages.

_____ 2. England's Parliament was divided into two parts, called the House of Lords and the House of Commons.

_____ 3. William the Conqueror brought feudalism to England, and set up a central tax system.

_____ 4. Chivalry was a code of conduct established for local lords and noblemen.

_____ 5. Today, France occupies the area once known as Gaul.

IDENTIFICATION *(6 points each)* Fill in the chart below showing the titles within the church's hierarchy. Write the letter of the most powerful role at the top, with the next most powerful underneath, and so on.

  a. bishop

  b. parish priest

  c. archbishop

  d. pope

  e. cardinal

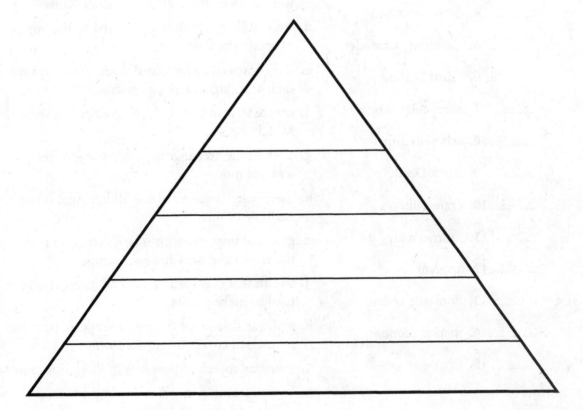

CHAPTER  14

Chapter Test Form C

Modern Chapter **5**

The High Middle Ages

MATCHING *(2 points each)* Place the letters of the descriptions next to the appropriate names and terms.

_____ **1.** Gothic

_____ **2.** middle class

_____ **3.** capital

_____ **4.** barter economy

_____ **5.** Children's Crusades

_____ **6.** Great Schism

_____ **7.** vernacular language

_____ **8.** scholasticism

_____ **9.** Black Death

_____ **10.** craft guild

_____ **11.** journeyman

_____ **12.** apprentice

_____ **13.** domestic system

_____ **14.** market economy

_____ **15.** Crusades

a. allows individuals to control land, labor and capital

b. the first stage of learning a trade

c. group made up of towns' guild members, who were between the nobles and the peasants

d. large military expedition, ordered by the pope, to regain the Holy Land

e. skilled workers who joined together to improve their working and living conditions

f. ornate style of architecture developed in the Middle Ages

g. allowed the exchange of goods and services without money

h. the woolen industry of the Middle Ages is one example of this

i. group of unprepared youth who tried to regain the Holy Land for Christian Europe

j. wealth that is earned, saved, and invested, and used to make profits

k. a plague that swept through Europe, in part due to unclean conditions in the towns

l. everyday speech of people with little education

m. level of training in which a young artisan is skilled and receives a wage

n. the bringing together of faith and reason

o. period of church history when as many as three popes ruled at one time

FILL IN THE BLANK *(3 points each)* Choose from the following list to complete each of the statements below.

Joan of Arc   Thomas Aquinas   Hundred Years' War
Babylonian Captivity   War of the Roses   Dante Alighieri
John Wycliffe   Geoffrey Chaucer

Chapter 14, Chapter Test Form C, continued

1. _____ believed that all people should have the opportunity to read the Bible for themselves.

2. *The Divine Comedy* was written by _____, who is considered by many to be the father of the Italian language.

3. The Dominican monk _____ is considered the greatest medieval philosopher.

4. The _____ began when Edward III of England laid claim to the French throne.

5. *The Canterbury Tales*, written by _____, used the stories of 30 traveling pilgrims to comment on English society.

6. _____ helped Charles VII win the French throne, before being accused of heresy, tortured, and burned at the stake by the English.

7. During the _____, people felt that the popes were being controlled by French kings.

8. The _____ was a fight for the English throne, fought between the House of York and the House of Lancaster.

TRUE/FALSE *(2 points each)* Mark each statement *T* if it is true or *F* if it is false.

_____ 1. The Hanseatic League set strict rules for trading.

_____ 2. The troy weight, used to measure gold and silver, is still in use today.

_____ 3. Lending money did not become a part of the banking system until after the Middle Ages.

_____ 4. Townspeople in Europe were given certain rights, written into each town's charter of liberty.

_____ 5. Merchant guilds took advantage of their members and members' families.

_____ 6. Serfs were known to escape to towns for freedom.

_____ 7. The growth of cities likely contributed to the spread of the Black Death.

_____ 8. Towns in the Middle Ages were much like the towns we live in today.

IDENTIFICATION *(5 points each)* Decide whether each of the following statements was or was not a result of the Crusades. Write the letter of each phrase in the correct box.

a. Trade diminished, making Europe more isolated.

b. The power of the popes diminished.

c. Feudalism came to an end.

d. Feudalism was strengthened.

e. Soldiers learned to undermine walls and use catapults.

f. Europeans were exposed to many new goods and ideas.

THE CRUSADES	
Was a Result	**Was Not a Result**

UNIT **3**

Modern Unit **1**

Unit Test Form C

The World in Transition

MATCHING *(2 points each)* Place the letters of the descriptions next to the appropriate names.

_____ **1.** Iconoclastic Controversy

_____ **2.** Qu'ran

_____ **3.** Hagia Sophia

_____ **4.** Muhammad

_____ **5.** Empress Wu

_____ **6.** Joan of Arc

_____ **7.** Moors

_____ **8.** Charlemagne

_____ **9.** Thomas Becket

_____ **10.** Li Bo

_____ **11.** Genghis Khan

_____ **12.** Magna Carta

_____ **13.** Thomas Aquinas

_____ **14.** Dante Alighieri

_____ **15.** Marco Polo

a. leader of the Tang dynasty

b. monk and philosopher who wrote a summary of medieval Christian thought

c. French heroine who followed her religious visions to help Charles VII defeat the English

d. Frankish ruler who worked to build a "new Rome," centered in France and Germany

e. Archbishop of Canterbury, who was murdered by Henry II's knights

f. writer, who is thought by many to be the father of the Italian language

g. believed to be the word of God, as given to Muhammad

h. Italian explorer who wrote of his experiences with Kublai Khan

i. debate over the use of religious symbols and images in worship

j. founder of Islam

k. document that outlined and protected the rights of England's people

l. fierce Mongol leader who acquired much land for his empire

m. a church built in Constantinople

n. Chinese poet who wrote of life's pleasures

o. Muslim people who settled in Spain

FILL IN THE BLANK *(3 points each)* Choose from the following list to complete each of the statements below.

feudalism	jihad	heresy
chivalry	scholasticism	*kamikaze*
mosques	domestic system	samurai
steppe		

1. Eastern European farmers found that black, fertile plains, called the

_____, were ideal for agriculture.

2. People accused of _____ risked excommunication from the church.

3. Under _____, local land owners granted the use of their land to others in return for loyalty, military assistance, and other services.

4. Knights were bound by a code of conduct, known as _____.

5. Muslims worshipped in _____, which had no religious pictures or statues.

6. The _____ refers to the manufacturing of goods in homes rather than in a shop or factory.

7. _____ was the name Japanese gave to a powerful typhoon that saved them from invasion by the Mongols.

8. Studying to become a _____ required strict training in the martial arts.

9. According to the Muslim religion, those who die in a _____ will be rewarded in heaven.

10. The struggle to bring together faith and reason is called _____.

TRUE/FALSE *(2 points each)* Mark each statement *T* if it is true or *F* if it is false.

_____ **1.** Buddhism was one of the most important religions in Japan.

_____ **2.** The Muslim Empire gained great wealth through trade.

_____ **3.** Several levels of authority existed in the church during the Middle Ages.

_____ **4.** The laws of the Roman Empire were never written in an organized form.

_____ **5.** The Crusades had little impact on the economy during the Middle Ages.

Unit 3, Unit Test Form C, continued

IDENTIFICATION *(3 points each)* Determine whether each of the phrases below describes the Byzantine Empire, the Islamic World, or the Civilizations of East Asia. Write the letter of each phrase in the correct box.

a. religious leader was Muhammad

b. practiced Zen Buddhism

c. led by Genghis Khan

d. religious text called the *Diamond Sutra*

e. built the Hagia Sophia

f. led by Abū Bakr

g. led by Ivan the Terrible

h. followed the Justinian Code

i. religious text called the Qu'ran

j. Christian church played an important role

Byzantine Empire	Islamic World	Civilizations of East Asia
_____	_____	_____
_____	_____	_____
_____	_____	_____
_____		

CHAPTER **15**   Chapter Test Form C

Modern Chapter **6**   **The Renaissance and Reformation**

MATCHING *(3 points each)* Place the letters of the descriptions next to the appropriate names.

_____ 1. Martin Luther

_____ 2. Johannes Gutenberg

_____ 3. John Calvin

_____ 4. Flemish school

_____ 5. perspective

_____ 6. Renaissance

_____ 7. theocracy

_____ 8. Francesco Petrarch

_____ 9. Reformation

_____ 10. Thomas More

a. artistic technique, used to create the illusion of depth on a flat surface

b. period of religious conflict that caused the church of Western Europe to split

c. a government that is lead by religious leaders

d. wrote *Utopia*, a work describing his view of an ideal society

e. felt strongly that the sale of indulgences was wrong

f. invented the printing press in Europe

g. style of painting that focused on using realistic details, especially lifelike facial expressions

h. teacher and writer best known for his sonnets written to Laura, an imaginary ideal woman

i. era in which many artistic and philosophical advances were made

j. French Protestant who founded a church that taught the idea of predestination

FILL IN THE BLANK *(3 points each)* Choose from the following list to complete each of the statements below.

humanists   Leonardo da Vinci   Michelangelo
Desiderius Erasmus   sects   standard of living

1. Students of grammar, history, poetry, and rhetoric were known as

_____.

2. _____, or groups of people with similar religious beliefs, often gathered to discuss religion.

3. _____ was an architect, an engineer, a painter, a sculptor, and a scientist.

4. _____ painted frescoes on the ceiling of the Sistine Chapel.

Chapter 15, Chapter Test Form C, continued

5. A humanist named _____ worked to combine ideas from Greek and Roman cultures with the ideas of Christianity.

TRUE/FALSE *(2 points each)* Mark each statement *T* if it is true or *F* if it is false.

_____ 1. During the Reformation, Northern European humanists believed that the church was too interested in making money.

_____ 2. A student with a classical education has studied only music and art.

_____ 3. The Renaissance began in Greece.

_____ 4. The invention of the printing press helped the ideas of the Renaissance spread into Northern Europe.

_____ 5. Townspeople during the Renaissance believed in witchcraft and spirits.

_____ 6. Indulgences were ornate pieces of religious jewelry that were sold to raise money for the church.

_____ 7. Martin Luther's beliefs made him very popular in the Catholic Church.

_____ 8. Reformers who broke from the Catholic Church were called Protestants, because they protested against the church.

_____ 9. Henry VIII formed the Anglican Church because the Catholic Church was not meeting his spiritual needs.

_____ 10. The Reformation and Counter Reformation led to a stronger interest in education.

Chapter 15, Chapter Test Form C, continued

IDENTIFICATION *(5 points each)* Decide whether each of the following people and ideas was involved in the Protestant Reformation or the Counter-Reformation. Write the letter of each phrase in the correct box.

a. Pope Paul III

b. Pope Leo X

c. the Inquisition

d. Huguenots

e. Ignatius de Loyola

f. indulgences

g. Calvinism

h. Jesuits

i. Council of Trent

j. Martin Luther

Protestant Reformation	Counter Reformation

Modern Chapter **7**

Chapter Test Form C
Exploration and Expansion

MATCHING *(2 points each)* Place the letters of the descriptions next to the appropriate names and terms.

_____ **1.** René Descartes	**a.** discovered the route to the Indian Ocean
_____ **2.** Andreas Vesalius	**b.** the use of experiments and mathematics to answer questions about the world
_____ **3.** Ferdinand Magellan	**c.** improved ways of doing business and changes in basic economic practices in Europe
_____ **4.** William of Orange	**d.** studied the human body and created a book with illustrations of his work
_____ **5.** Francis Bacon	**e.** Portuguese explorer known as "The Navigator"
_____ **6.** Scientific Revolution	**f.** believed that scientific theories could be developed only through observation
_____ **7.** Prince Henry	**g.** sailed to the West Indies in his search for a shorter trade route to Asia
_____ **8.** Bartolomeu Dias	**h.** agreement between Spain and Portugal regarding the division of newly discovered lands
_____ **9.** Christopher Columbus	**i.** one of the first explorers to believe that the New World was not part of Asia
_____ **10.** Queen Isabella	**j.** wrote "I think, therefore I am."
_____ **11.** Francisco Pizarro	**k.** exchange of products, animals, plants, and diseases between the Old and New worlds
_____ **12.** Treaty of Tordesillas	**l.** destroyed many Aztec and Incan statues and temples for the gold and silver they contained
_____ **13.** Amerigo Vespucci	**m.** Spanish ruler who financed the voyages of Columbus
_____ **14.** Columbian Exchange	**n.** led the Calvinist Netherlands to independence from Catholic Spain
_____ **15.** Commercial Revolution	**o.** named the Pacific Ocean

FILL IN THE BLANK *(3 points each)* Choose from the following list to complete each of the statements below.

tariff	scientific method	joint-stock companies
guerrilla warfare	subsidy	mercantilism
alchemists	triangular trade	favorable balance of trade
heliocentric theory		

1. The _____ argues that the sun is the center of the universe.

2. Organizations called _____ raised large sums of money for exploration by selling shares of a business to investors, who received a share of the profits.

3. When a country is able to sell more goods than it buys from another country, it is said to have a _____.

4. A tax placed on goods imported into a country is called a _____.

5. The process of making observations, conducting experiments, and drawing conclusions is known as the _____.

6. _____ tried to control the natural world through the use of spells and magic.

7. _____ is an economic theory stating that a government should try to increase its wealth by gaining more silver and gold.

8. In the _____ system, merchants shipped goods to Africa to trade for slaves, who were then sent to the Americas to work on sugar plantations.

9. Grant money given to individuals by the government to finance new businesses is called a _____.

10. An unconventional style of battle, called _____, uses techniques such as small, quick raids to confuse an opposing army.

TRUE/FALSE *(3 points each)* Mark each statement *T* if it is true or *F* if it is false.

_____ **1.** Europeans tried to enslave Native Americans first, but found it too difficult and turned to Africa for slaves instead.

_____ **2.** The astrolabe was a more effective navigational tool than the compass.

_____ **3.** Colonies played a major role in the rise of mercantilism.

_____ **4.** Religious freedom was the only reason people decided to explore new lands.

_____ **5.** Many Native Americans died as a result of being exposed to diseases such as smallpox.

Chapter 16, Chapter Test Form C, continued

IDENTIFICATION *(5 points each)* Match each law or scientific discovery with the scientist who made the discovery. Write the letter of each name or phrase in the correct box.

a. observed the sun and the planets using a telescope

b. geocentric theory

c. Nicolaus Copernicus

d. Johannes Kepler

e. law of universal gravitation

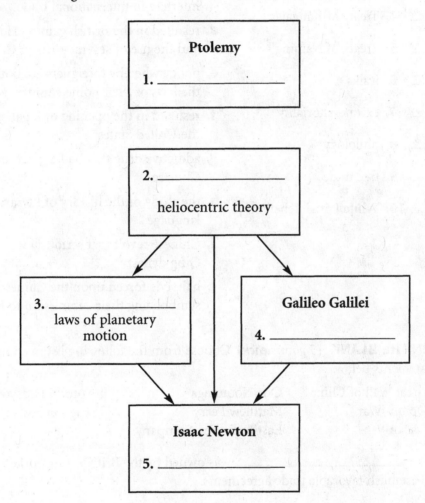

Ptolemy

1. _____

2. _____

heliocentric theory

3. _____
laws of planetary
motion

Galileo Galilei

4. _____

Isaac Newton

5. _____

CHAPTER 17

Modern Chapter 8

Chapter Test Form C

Asia in Transition

MATCHING *(3 points each)* Place the letters of the descriptions next to the appropriate names and terms.

_____ **1.** opium

_____ **2.** Taiping Rebellion

_____ **3.** queue

_____ **4.** Treaty of Kangawa

_____ **5.** Treaty of Nanjing

_____ **6.** junks

_____ **7.** extraterritoriality

_____ **8.** philology

_____ **9.** free trade

_____ **10.** White Lotus Rebellion

a. name given by Europeans to the Chinese ships

b. revolt led by a Buddhist cult in protest of Chinese government inefficiency

c. belief that governments should not restrict or interfere in international trade

d. resulted in the British gaining Hong Kong and the use of several ports in China

e. policy whereby foreigners are bound only by the laws of their home country

f. resulted in the opening of Japanese ports to the United States

g. addictive drug that had a great impact on the Chinese

h. the study of the history of literature and language

i. Chinese revolt that seriously weakened the Qing dynasty

j. hairstyle forced upon the Chinese, symbolizing their submission to Manchu rule

FILL IN THE BLANK *(3 points each)* Choose from the following list to complete each of the statements below.

Great Wall of China   Oda Nobunaga   Toyotomi Hideyoshi
Opium War   Matthew Perry   Tokugawa Ieyasu
Hsüan-yeh   East India Tea Company

1. The _____ was owned by the British, and worked with China to establish favorable trade agreements.

2. The _____ ended with the Chinese being forced to open their country for trade with the British.

3. _____ ended the Ashikaga shogunate and became the first of the powerful overlords to rule in Japan.

4. The capital of Edo, the city that is now Tokyo, was established by

_____.

5. The powerful naval commander, _____, negotiated the treaty that opened Japan for trade with the United States.

6. _____ carried out a "sword hunt" to disarm peasants, preventing them from becoming warriors.

7. _____ was a Qing ruler who was not Chinese, but adopted the Chinese culture.

8. The Ming Dynasty strengthened the _____ to protect China's northern borders.

TRUE/FALSE *(2 points each)* Mark each statement *T* if it is true or *F* if it is false.

_____ **1.** Even though they had well-built ships, the Chinese chose to stop financing naval explorations.

_____ **2.** The Chinese grew some crops that were brought from the Americas.

_____ **3.** The Chinese were willing trade partners to many European countries.

_____ **4.** Opium played an important role in the history of China.

_____ **5.** China and Japan had similar views on foreign trade.

_____ **6.** Portuguese missionaries were not able to convert many Japanese to Christianity.

_____ **7.** China and Japan both adopted the Confucian ideal of social classes.

_____ **8.** In Japan, anyone who went through training could serve as a samurai.

Chapter 17, Chapter Test Form C, continued

IDENTIFICATION *(5 points each)* Place the following events from Chinese history in the order in which they occurred. Write the letter of each phrase on the appropriate line.

a. Opium War

b. Ming dynasty rules

c. East India Tea Company trades with China

d. Qing dynasty rules

e. White Lotus Rebellion

f. China forced to sign "unequal" treaties

1. _____

2. _____

3. _____

4. _____

5. _____

6. _____

CHAPTER **18**

Chapter Test Form C

Modern Chapter **9**

Islamic Empires in Asia

MATCHING *(3 points each)* Place the letters of the descriptions next to the appropriate names and terms.

_____ **1.** Osman

_____ **2.** 'Abbās

_____ **3.** Akbar

_____ **4.** Taj Mahal

_____ **5.** Aurangzeb

_____ **6.** Esmā'īl

_____ **7.** Mehmed II

_____ **8.** Timur

_____ **9.** Rajputs

_____ **10.** Sikh

a. Turko-Mongol leader who claimed to be a descendent of Genghis Khan

b. religion that grew from the blending of Hindu and Muslim cultures

c. Safavid leader who built the beautiful capital city of Eşfahān

d. brought all of modern Iran and part of present-day Iraq under his control

e. Indian warrior princes whose challenge of the Turkish Muslims left India open for attack

f. believing himself to be a divine ruler, he established a creed called the Divine Faith

g. ghazi leader whose tribe members became known as the Ottomans

h. ruthless leader who imprisoned his father and killed his brother to gain control

i. architectural wonder, built as a tomb for Shah Jahān's wife

j. Ottoman sultan who changed the name of Constantinople to Istanbul

FILL IN THE BLANK *(2 points each)* Choose from the following list to complete each of the statements below.

kizilbash   millets   Janissaries
ghazis   reaya

1. A military group, known as the _____ was developed by the Safavids to gain political power.

2. Separate religious communities, called _____, were allowed to govern themselves under the rule of the Ottoman Empire.

3. Ottoman society was divided into two main groups: the ruling class and the

_____.

Chapter 18, Chapter Test Form C, continued

4. The _____ were a group of young war captives and Christian slaves trained to serve the Ottoman soldiers.

5. _____, or warriors for Islam, were the first Ottomans.

TRUE/FALSE *(3 points each)* Mark each statement *T* if it is true or *F* if it is false.

_____ 1. The Ottoman army, made up of trained slaves, came to be a powerful political force.

_____ 2. At one time, the Ottoman empire stretched into eastern Europe, western Asia, and northern Africa.

_____ 3. Grand viziers were the supreme rulers of the Ottoman society.

_____ 4. The Ottoman empire is still a powerful force in the Republic of Turkey.

_____ 5. The Safavids and the Ottomans fought over the control of key territories.

_____ 6. The Safavid Empire was the first to train slaves as military troops.

_____ 7. Carpet weaving became a major industry during the Safavid Empire.

_____ 8. Bābur established the Mughal Empire.

_____ 9. Akbar was intolerant of religions other than his own.

_____ 10. Aurangzeb was a devout Sunni Muslim, and strictly followed Islamic law.

IDENTIFICATION *(3 points each)* Fill in the chart. Place the letter of the correct description into its proper category below.

  a. sultan

  b. Sikh faith was formed

  c. many religions, organized into millets

  d. Akbar

  e. 'Abbās

  f. shah

  g. emperor

  h. Shi'ah Muslim

  i. Süleyman

	Ottoman	Safavid	Mughal
Title of ruler			
Famous Ruler			
Prevalent religion			

UNIT **4**

Modern Unit **2**

Unit Test Form C

The Age of Exploration and Expansion

MATCHING *(3 points each)* Place the letters of the descriptions next to the appropriate terms.

_____ **1.** Shah ʿAbbās

_____ **2.** Aurangzeb

_____ **3.** Timur

_____ **4.** Toyotomi Hideyoshi

_____ **5.** Matthew Perry

_____ **6.** Ferdinand Magellan

_____ **7.** Amerigo Verspucci

_____ **8.** Isaac Newton

_____ **9.** John Calvin

_____ **10.** Martin Luther

a. his Protestant church emphasized predestination

b. explorer who named the Pacific Ocean

c. proposed the law of universal gravitation

d. believed the sale of indulgences was wrong

e. built the beautiful capital city of Eşfahān

f. claimed to be a descendent of Genghis Khan; led Mongols to victory over the Ottomans

g. killed his brother and imprisoned his father to become emperor

h. American naval commander who negotiated the treaty opening Japanese ports for trade

i. Japanese overlord who created a policy that prevented peasants from becoming warriors

j. Italian navigator whose claims of finding a New World inspired a German mapmaker to call the new land America

FILL IN THE BLANK *(3 points each)* Choose from the following list to complete each of the statements below.

mercantilism	humanists	reaya
guerrilla warfare	Reformation	Treaty of Kanagawa
scientific method	Flemish School	White Lotus Rebellion
ghazis		

1. The _____ resulted in the opening of Japanese ports to America.

2. A period of religious conflict that caused the division of the church in Western Europe is known as the _____.

3. _____ were people who studied history, grammar, poetry, and rhetoric during the Renaissance.

4. The first Ottomans were Turkish soldiers called _____.

5. A style of battle known as _____ uses tactics such as small, quick raids meant to confuse the opposing army.

6. The process of making observations, conducting experiments, and drawing conclusions is known as the _____.

7. A struggle known as the _____ involved a Buddhist cult and the Chinese government.

8. _____ is an economic theory stating that a government should try to increase its wealth by gaining silver and gold.

9. The ruling class and the _____ were the two main groups in the Ottoman society.

10. A style of painting that focused on the use of realistic details, especially lifelike facial expressions, was called the _____.

TRUE/FALSE *(2 points each)* Mark each statement *T* if it is true or *F* if it is false.

_____ **1.** Leonardo da Vinci painted frescoes on the ceiling of the Sistine Chapel.

_____ **2.** Reformers who broke from the Catholic Church were called Protestants, because they protested against the church.

_____ **3.** The Sikh faith was a blending of Hindu and Muslim religions, intending to unify the two groups.

_____ **4.** The Ottomans used a group of trained slave-warriors to become a powerful political force.

_____ **5.** The Taj Mahal was built to serve as a tomb.

_____ **6.** The Columbian Exchange was not equal, in that the New World did not benefit as much as the Old World.

_____ **7.** Explorers were motivated only by a desire for wealth.

_____ **8.** The rectangular trade pattern involved the exchange of slaves and raw materials between the Old and New Worlds.

_____ **9.** Chinese ships were called junks by the Europeans.

_____ **10.** The Opium War led to improved trade with Japan.

Unit 4, Unit Test Form C, continued

IDENTIFICATION *(2 points each)* Complete the diagram about the Ottoman and the Portuguese Empires by writing the letter of each item in the appropriate column.

a. set up sugar plantations on islands off the coast of Africa

b. used slaves

c. organized religious communities, called millets

d. signed a treaty with Spain to divide new lands

e. divided into a ruling class and subjects

f. explored westward into the Atlantic

g. fought the Safavid Empire

h. expansion was a primary goal

i. used slave-warriors

j. used ships to open sea routes for trade

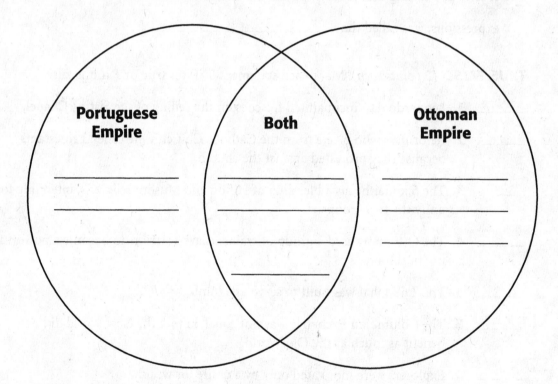

CHAPTER 19

Modern Chapter **10**

Chapter Test Form C

Monarchs of Europe

MATCHING *(2 points each)* Place the letters of the descriptions next to the appropriate names.

_____ **1.** Mary Queen of Scots

_____ **2.** Catherine the Great

_____ **3.** Maria Theresa

_____ **4.** Elizabeth I

_____ **5.** Mary I

a. inherited Austria and other Habsburg lands, despite the law stating land must go to a male

b. English queen whose leadership made the country into a great world power

c. Queen of England; known for her bloody elimination of non-Catholics

d. led the Russian Empire after the death of her husband; supporter of the arts

e. Catholic queen who was in line for the English throne, but was beheaded

FILL IN THE BLANK *(3 points each)* Choose from the following list to complete each of the statements below.

balance of power   burgesses   Pragmatic Sanction
gentry   service nobility   Diplomatic Revolution
Puritans   intendants   Spanish Armada
divine right of kings

1. The _____ were the French monarchy's representatives in the provinces that made up France.

2. The palace of Versailles was important to Louis XIV because it symbolized his power and belief in the _____.

3. Many European nations wanted a _____, in which countries have equal strength to prevent any one country from dominating the others.

4. The _____ were landowners who had social position but no titles.

5. An agreement among European rulers allowing for the rule of Maria Theresa was known as the _____.

6. The _____ was a "reversal of alliances" resulting from concerns over the balance of power after the War of the Austrian Succession.

7. The _____ was a large fleet of impressive ships that were badly damaged during a conflict with England.

Chapter 19, Chapter Test Form C, continued

8. The _____ were persecuted by the Tudors for criticizing the Anglican Church.

9. Merchants and professionals known as _____ served in the House of Commons.

10. A political system in which an individual's rank depends on the performance of

government service is called _____.

TRUE/FALSE *(3 points each)* Mark each statement *T* if it is true or *F* if it is false.

_____ **1.** Cardinal Richelieu worked against Henry IV to weaken the French throne.

_____ **2.** Versailles is the name given to a church built for King Louis XIV.

_____ **3.** Louis XIV was nicknamed the Sun King.

_____ **4.** The Romanov czars ruled Russia for three centuries.

_____ **5.** Religious groups known as the Old Believers tried to weaken the power of the Russian czar.

_____ **6.** Peter the Great ruled England until 1725.

_____ **7.** Poland was divided among other countries in a series of actions known as the Partitions.

_____ **8.** A period of peace existed for a time in Europe, because of the heavy cost of many years of war.

_____ **9.** Some English rulers favored the Anglican Church, while others preferred the Catholic Church.

_____ **10.** Puritans were important leaders in the Anglican Church.

Chapter 19, Chapter Test Form C, continued

IDENTIFICATION *(5 points each)* Match each treaty and treaty provision with the correct war by placing each of the following letters in the correct box on the chart.

   a. Treaty of Westphalia

   b. Treaty of Utrecht

   c. Treaty of Paris

   d. France received Alsace

   e. Prussia received Silesia

   f. Great Britain received French lands in North America

War	Treaty	Provision
Thirty Years' War	1. _____	1. _____
War of the Spanish Succession	2. _____	2. _____
Seven Years' War	3. _____	3. _____

CHAPTER **20** Chapter Test Form C

Modern Chapter 11   **Enlightenment and Revolution in England and America**

MATCHING *(2 points each)* Place the letters of the descriptions next to the appropriate names and terms.

_____ **1.** Charles I

_____ **2.** Oliver Cromwell

_____ **3.** Cavaliers

_____ **4.** Roundheads

_____ **5.** Whigs

_____ **6.** William III

_____ **7.** John Locke

_____ **8.** John Cabot

_____ **9.** Sir Francis Drake

_____ **10.** Voltaire

_____ **11.** Denis Diderot

_____ **12.** Patriots

_____ **13.** Loyalists

_____ **14.** Benjamin Franklin

_____ **15.** George Washington

a. negotiated the Treaty of Paris at the end of the American Revolution

b. commander of the American troops during the Revolution

c. English political party that supported a strong Parliament

d. English sea captain who was the first to claim North American land for England

e. Protestant Dutch prince married to Mary, daughter of James II

f. American colonists who wanted independence from England

g. reigning king during England's Civil War

h. supported Parliament during the English Civil War

i. the first English sea captain to sail around the world

j. American colonists who wanted to remain an English colony

k. supported the monarchy during the English Civil War

l. edited *The Encyclopedia*, a set of 28 books that describe the ideas of the Enlightenment

m. wrote "I [may] disapprove of what you say, but I will defend to the death your right to say it."

n. Puritan leader who defeated an English king and established a commonwealth in England

o. English philosopher who believed that people had the right to life, liberty, and property

Chapter 20, Chapter Test Form C, continued

FILL IN THE BLANK *(2 points each)* Choose from the following list to complete each of the statements below.

Bill of Rights   Rump Parliament   Navigation Act of 1651
sea dogs   mercantilism   Petition of Right
Habeas Corpus Act   Long Parliament   federal system of government
prime minister

1. Parliament presented King Charles I with the _____, a document meant to limit the power of the king.

2. The passing of the _____ led to war with the Dutch.

3. The _____ removed the king and the House of Lords from power.

4. The _____ met regularly for 20 years, and kept the king from raising taxes on his own.

5. Parliament passed the _____ to protect individuals from being arrested without cause.

6. Sir Robert Walpole was England's first _____.

7. English traders and pirates, called _____, explored unknown land and helped England defeat the Spanish Armada.

8. The British policy of _____ angered many colonists because it limited their ability to trade.

9. A _____ gives significant power to a central government, while leaving some power to each state.

10. A statement of ten rights of individuals, called the _____, was added to the U.S. Constitution.

TRUE/FALSE *(2 points each)* Mark each statement *T* if it is true or *F* if it is false.

_____ **1.** Oliver Cromwell and his New Model Army defeated King Charles in the English Civil War.

_____ **2.** After Oliver Cromwell's death, his son Richard strengthened the English commonwealth.

_____ **3.** Charles II's ascension to power was called the Restoration.

_____ **4.** Different ideas about who should be the next king led to the formation of two political parties, the Whigs and the Tories.

_____ **5.** William III and Mary II led England to defeat the Dutch during the Glorious Revolution.

_____ **6.** Under the British system of limited constitutional monarchy, the king has absolute power.

_____ **7.** Plymouth was the first permanent British settlement in North America.

_____ **8.** Most English colonies allowed self-government, even though the king had ultimate authority.

_____ **9.** The French and Indian War left Britain with large debts that they passed on to the colonists in the form of increased taxes.

_____ **10.** The Articles of Confederation created a weak central government, leaving most of the power to each state.

IDENTIFICATION *(3 points each)* Put the following events in order of their occurrence. Write the letter of each phrase next to the correct numbered space, from the earliest to the most recent.

a. Articles of Confederation

b. Charles I is executed

c. the Long Parliament meets

d. English Bill of Rights

e. Glorious Revolution

f. Sugar Act and Stamp Act

g. American Revolution

h. England and Scotland are united, forming Great Britain

i. English Civil War

j. Restoration

1. _____   **6.** _____

2. _____   **7.** _____

3. _____   **8.** _____

4. _____   **9.** _____

5. _____   **10.** _____

 **CHAPTER 21**

Modern Chapter **12**

Chapter Test Form C

The French Revolution and Napoléon

MATCHING *(3 points each)* Place the letters of the descriptions next to the appropriate terms.

_____ **1.** Louis XV

_____ **2.** Marie-Antoinette

_____ **3.** Olympe de Gouges

_____ **4.** conservatives

_____ **5.** radicals

_____ **6.** Napoléon Bonaparte

_____ **7.** Concordat

_____ **8.** nationalism

_____ **9.** indemnity

_____ **10.** Prince Metternich

a. agreement between the French government and the church allowing religious freedom

b. Austrian wife of Louis XV

c. political group in favor of a government in which the king has limited authority

d. financial reward given to compensate for damages

e. French general who led a coup d'état and became emperor

f. woman who unsuccessfully worked to gain equal rights for women and men

g. king, whose 59-year reign added greatly to the French national debt

h. Austrian who believed in the absolute monarchy and was influential in European politics

i. political group that wanted to create a republic to replace the king

j. love of one's country

FILL IN THE BLANK *(3 points each)* Choose from the following list to complete each of the statements below.

émigrés   bourgeoisie   universal manhood suffrage
Louis XVI   legitimacy   scorched-earth policy
Directory   reactionaries   liberalism
Reign of Terror

1. The French middle class were called the _____.

2. _____ called a meeting of all three Estates of the Estates General, hoping to gain approval for new taxes.

3. Nobles who fled France during the French Revolution because they feared for their lives were called _____.

4. Delegates to the National Convention that met to create a constitution were elected by _____, in which every adult male could vote.

5. The _____ was a period of time when the National Convention used any means necessary to end opposition to the republic.

6. The constitution created by the National Convention in 1795 formed a new government, called the _____, which lasted only four years.

7. The Russian military practiced a _____ against Napoléon, burning or destroying crops and everything else the Grand Army might need.

8. The Congress of Vienna followed the rule of _____, restoring all former ruling families to their thrones.

9. The movement known as _____ believed in individual rights and the rule of law.

10. Following the Napoléonic Era, _____ wanted to undo changes made to government and return things to the way they were before.

TRUE/FALSE *(2 points each)* Mark each statement *T* if it is true or *F* if it is false.

_____ **1.** French society was divided into four estates, or classes.

_____ **2.** During the French Revolution, France was divided into eighty-three departments.

_____ **3.** The National Convention created a Committee of Public Safety to direct the army against foreign invasion.

_____ **4.** Under a plebiscite, people could only vote for or against an idea, and could not suggest any changes.

_____ **5.** Prince Metternich of Austria worked to bring liberal ideas into France.

Chapter 21, Chapter Test Form C, continued

IDENTIFICATION *(3 points each)* Place the letter of the correct description into its proper category below.

a. Roman Catholic clergy

b. two percent of the population

c. paid heavy taxes

d. nobility

e. bourgeoisie

f. held fifteen percent of the land

g. peasants

h. held high positions in government

i. one percent of the population

First Estate	Second Estate	Third Estate
_____	_____	_____
_____	_____	_____
_____	_____	_____

UNIT 5

Modern Unit **3**

Unit Test Form C

From Absolutism to Revolution

MATCHING *(3 points each)* Place the letters of the descriptions next to the appropriate terms.

_____ **1.** Bill of Rights

_____ **2.** balance of power

_____ **3.** service nobility

_____ **4.** intendants

_____ **5.** Whigs

_____ **6.** Patriots

_____ **7.** liberalism

_____ **8.** Reign of Terror

_____ **9.** bourgeoisie

_____ **10.** reactionaries

a. the French middle class

b. American colonists who wanted independence from England

c. when countries have equal strength, insuring that no one country becomes too strong

d. people who oppose change, and want to undo some changes already in place

e. movement that believes in individual rights and the rule of law

f. individuals who represented the French monarchy in the provinces

g. period when the National Convention used any means necessary to end opposition to the republic

h. ten rights of individuals added to the United States Constitution

i. political system where rank depends on the performance of a government service

j. English political party that supported a strong Parliament

FILL IN THE BLANK *(3 points each)* Choose from the following list to complete each of the statements below.

Oliver Cromwell   Sir Francis Drake   Catherine the Great
John Cabot   John Locke   Napoléon Bonaparte
Benjamin Franklin   Maria Theresa

1. _____ led the Russian Empire after the death of her husband, greatly expanding Russian territory.

2. The rights to life, liberty, and property were beliefs of a philosopher named

_____.

Unit 5, Unit Test Form C, continued

3. _____ negotiated the Treaty of Paris to end the American Revolution.

4. The French general _____ became emperor of France.

5. Austria was inherited by _____, even though the law stated land can be inherited only by males.

6. _____ was a Puritan leader who defeated an English king and established a commonwealth in England.

7. _____ was the first English sea captain to sail around the world.

8. _____ was the first English sea captain to claim land in North America for England.

TRUE/FALSE *(2 points each)* Mark each statement *T* if it is true or *F* if it is false.

_____ **1.** The Navigation Act of 1651 led to a war between England and the Dutch.

_____ **2.** The Articles of Confederation created a strong government which still exists today.

_____ **3.** The Glorious Revolution was a bloodless transfer of power in the English monarchy.

_____ **4.** Prince Metternich of Austria worked to bring liberal ideas into France.

_____ **5.** The First Estate was made up of the clergy of the Roman Catholic Church.

_____ **6.** Puritans were leaders in the Anglican Church.

_____ **7.** An agreement among European leaders allowing Catherine the Great to rule was known as Pragmatic Sanction.

_____ **8.** Mary I was known as "Bloody Mary" because she executed many clergy who would not follow the laws of the Catholic Church.

Unit 5, Unit Test Form C, continued

IDENTIFICATION *(2 points each)* Fill in the chart below by determining whether each statement or person is associated with England or with France. Write the letter of each phrase in the correct column.

a. Marie-Antoinette

b. Concordat

c. Whigs

d. Versailles

e. Habeas Corpus Act

f. Prime Minister

g. Sir Robert Walpole

h. the Directory

i. Olympe de Gouges

j. Roundheads

ENGLAND	FRANCE
_____	_____
_____	_____
_____	_____
_____	_____
_____	_____

CHAPTER **22**

Modern Chapter **13**

Chapter Test Form C

The Industrial Revolution

MATCHING *(2 points each)* Place the letters of the descriptions next to the appropriate terms.

_____ **1.** Jethro Tull

_____ **2.** Eli Whitney

_____ **3.** James Watt

_____ **4.** Robert Fulton

_____ **5.** Samuel Morse

_____ **6.** Henry Ford

_____ **7.** J.P. Morgan

_____ **8.** Adam Smith

_____ **9.** Jeremy Bentham

_____ **10.** Karl Marx

a. patented the modern steam engine

b. used the assembly line to produce automobiles

c. invented the seed drill

d. theory of utilitarianism

e. invented the telegraph

f. founder of United States Steel Company

g. invented the cotton gin

h. considered the founder of classical economics

i. wrote the *Communist Manifesto*

j. first to build a profitable steamboat

FILL IN THE BLANK *(3 points each)* Choose from the following list to complete each of the statements below.

middle class   strike   collective bargaining
vulcanization   tenements   interchangeable parts
capitalism   socialism   corporations
mechanization

1. Charles Goodyear invented the process of _____, which makes rubber less sticky and easier to work with.

2. _____ is the use of automatic machinery to increase the amount of material produced.

3. Factory workers did not make much money and often lived in crowded

   _____ with many other people.

4. The Industrial Revolution led to the rise of the _____, which is based on economic standing rather than birth.

5. Under a system of _____, businesses are privately owned and operated.

6. The development of _____ led to the use of an assembly line and mass production.

7. New _____ sold stock to investors in order to raise the money needed to start a business.

8. Workers would often _____ to protest poor wages or working conditions.

9. Union representatives and management worked together to agree on wages, hours, and working conditions using a process called _____.

10. The government owns and operates businesses under the economic system called _____.

TRUE/FALSE *(2 points each)* Mark each statement *T* if it is true or *F* if it is false.

_____ 1. The enclosure movement made life on small family farms easier.

_____ 2. The rise of the factory system led to more women and children going to work.

_____ 3. A factory worker's wages depended on the cost of production, the availability of labor, and the wages of other workers.

_____ 4. The Factory Act of 1833 banned women and children from working in factories.

_____ 5. Communism is also known as democratic socialism.

Chapter 22, Chapter Test Form C, continued

IDENTIFICATION *(5 points each)* Place the letter of the correct description under the appropriate movement.

   a. unions

   b. proletariat

   c. Friedrich Engles

   d. Jethro Tull

   e. mechanization

   f. factors of production

   g. crop rotation

   h. J.P. Morgan

   i. communism

   j. cartels

AGRICULTURAL REVOLUTION	INDUSTRIAL REVOLUTION	CAPITALISM	SOCIALISM
_____	_____	_____	_____
_____	_____	_____	_____
		_____	

CHAPTER 23

Chapter Test Form C

Modern Chapter **14**

Life in the Industrial Age

MATCHING *(2 points each)* Place the letters of the descriptions next to the appropriate terms.

_____ **1.** Thomas Edison

_____ **2.** Wilbur and Orville Wright

_____ **3.** Charles Darwin

_____ **4.** Alexander Fleming

_____ **5.** Mark Twain

_____ **6.** Jane Addams

_____ **7.** Grimm brothers

_____ **8.** Ivan Pavlov

_____ **9.** Sigmund Freud

_____ **10.** Pierre and Marie Curie

_____ **11.** Dmitry Mendeleyev

_____ **12.** Auguste Comte

_____ **13.** Albert Einstein

_____ **14.** Alexander Graham Bell

_____ **15.** Guglielmo Marconi

a. invented the telegraph, which was used in wireless ship-to-shore communications

b. discovered penicillin

c. created a system for transmitting electricity from a central powerhouse to other places

d. famous for his theory of evolution

e. patented the telephone in 1876

f. regionalist writer who described life along the Mississippi River

g. first to fly successfully in a powered airplane

h. one of the founders of sociology

i. introduced the idea of the unconscious as a determining factor in human behavior

j. opened Hull House, which became a model for community service centers in the United States

k. collected well-known fairy tales

l. had a major impact in the field of physics with his equation, $E = mc^2$

m. determined that human actions can be changed by training

n. created the first version of the periodic table of elements

o. discovered "radioactivity," or the breakdown and release of energy from an element

FILL IN THE BLANK *(3 points each)* Choose from the following list to complete each of the statements below.

romanticism	suburbs	aerodynamics
emigration	dynamo	social Darwinism
bobbies	petroleum	psychiatry
genetics		

1. _____ is the study and treatment of mental illness.

2. As cities grew larger, residential areas on the outskirts called

_____ began to develop.

Chapter 23, Chapter Test Form C, continued

3. An artistic movement in which people valued emotion and instinct above reason is

known as _____.

4. The science of _____ involves the way air moves around objects.

5. Gregor Mendel founded _____, the study of how inborn characteristics are passed from generation to generation.

6. The first electric generator, or _____, was developed by Michael Faraday.

7. Between 1870 and 1900 more than 10 million people left Europe for the United

States in a mass _____, or movement of people away from their native land.

8. _____ is the thought that wealthy people possess abilities that are superior to the abilities of people who are poor.

9. A permanent police force, with officers called "_____," was established in London by Sir Robert Peel.

10. Crude oil used to power cars, airplanes, and ships is known as

_____.

TRUE/FALSE *(3 points each)* Mark each statement *T* if it is true or *F* if it is false.

_____ **1.** The first electric light bulbs burned for many months.

_____ **2.** Electric motors were not practical for moving vehicles because they could not be removed from their power supplies.

_____ **3.** Until the late 1800s, about 50 percent of all people born died within the first five years of life.

_____ **4.** Louis Pasteur was able to explain why vaccines were effective in preventing serious disease.

_____ **5.** Scientists were able to trace the spread of malaria and yellow fever to the fleas on rats.

_____ **6.** The study of politics began in the 1800s.

_____ **7.** Improvements in medicine, sanitation, and food distribution led to an increase in the population of the United States.

Chapter 23, Chapter Test Form C, continued

_____ **8.** The rise of the factory system contributed greatly to rural growth.

_____ **9.** The spread of education resulted in an increase in demand for newspapers.

_____ **10.** In the mid-1800s, writers and artists began to focus on more realistic subject material.

IDENTIFICATION *(5 points each)* Determine whether each of the advancements below improved the area of physical, biological, or social science. Place the letter of the advancement into its proper category below.

a. study of economics

b. development of antisepsis

c. process of psychoanalysis

d. quantum theory

e. theory of evolution

f. theory of relativity

PHYSICAL SCIENCE	BIOLOGICAL SCIENCE	SOCIAL SCIENCE
_____	_____	_____
_____	_____	_____

CHAPTER 24   Chapter Test Form C

Modern Chapter 15   **The Age of Reform**

MATCHING (*2 points each*) Place the letters of the descriptions next to the appropriate terms.

_____ **1.** Lord Durham

_____ **2.** suffrage

_____ **3.** Benjamin Disraeli

_____ **4.** Otto von Bismarck

_____ **5.** secede

_____ **6.** Florence Nightingale

_____ **7.** Lucretia Mott

_____ **8.** creoles

_____ **9.** mulattoes

_____ **10.** mestizos

a. head of the Prussian government during the Franco-Prussian War

b. white people born in the Latin American colonies

c. conservative leader who served two terms as British prime minister

d. American suffragette

e. people with American Indian and European ancestry

f. the right to vote

g. British liberal sent to reform Canada's government

h. introduced professional nursing

i. people of European and African ancestry

j. to withdraw from a union

FILL IN THE BLANK (*2 points each*) Choose from the following list to complete each of the statements below.

haciendas   suffragettes   sectionalism
anarchists   coalitions

1. Women who campaigned for the right to vote were known as

_____.

2. Competition between different parts of the United States resulted in

_____, which eventually led to the Civil War.

3. People who distrusted formal government, or _____, used terrorist means to overthrow European government.

4. French political groups often formed _____ to support a common cause.

5. Wealthy colonists living in Spanish America often resided in

_____.

Chapter 24, Chapter Test Form C, continued

TRUE/FALSE (*3 points each*) Mark each statement *T* if it is true or *F* if it is false.

_____ **1.** Liberalism is a philosophy that supports the absolute rule of a monarch.

_____ **2.** The Reform Bill of 1832 increased the number of people who could vote.

_____ **3.** Britain's conservative party was made up primarily of wealthy landowners.

_____ **4.** When 5,000 males lived in a territory of the United States, Congress would grant that territory statehood.

_____ **5.** The United States purchased the Louisiana Territory from Spain.

_____ **6.** The United States was composed of three major sections: the North, the South, and the West.

_____ **7.** Spain and Portugal used their Latin American colonies as a source of gold and silver, as well as a place to market their goods.

_____ **8.** Charles III of Spain took steps to improve the quality of life for colonists living in Latin America.

_____ **9.** The only successful slave revolt in history led to the creation of Haiti, the first independent Latin American country.

_____ **10.** The Monroe Doctrine stated that the United States had the right to purchase the Louisiana Territory.

IDENTIFICATION *(5 points each)* Identify the terms and people associated with reforms in each of the following regions. Place each letter in the correct column.

a. Catholic Emancipation Act

b. Elizabeth Cady Stanton

c. Revolution of 1848

d. peninsulares

e. sectionalism

f. Communards

g. William Gladstone

h. Toussaint-Louverture

i. Abraham Lincoln

j. Simón Bolívar

k. The Third Republic

l. chartists

m. Louis Philippe

n. Northwest Ordinance

o. Emmeline Pankhurst

GREAT BRITAIN	UNITED STATES	FRANCE	LATIN AMERICA
_____	_____	_____	_____
_____	_____	_____	_____
_____	_____	_____	_____
_____	_____	_____	

CHAPTER 25

Modern Chapter **16**

Chapter Test Form C

Nationalism in Europe

MATCHING (*3 points each*) Place the letters of the descriptions next to the appropriate names and terms.

_____ **1.** Giuseppe Mazzini

_____ **2.** Victor Emmanuel II

_____ **3.** Camillo Benso di Cavour

_____ **4.** Bundesrat

_____ **5.** Reichstag

_____ **6.** William I

_____ **7.** autocrat

_____ **8.** Alexander II

_____ **9.** Magyars

_____ **10.** Francis Joseph I

a. the upper house of the German legislature

b. a leader who holds absolute power

c. king of Sardinia, would become king of a unified Italy

d. czar of Russia who paid attention to public opinion

e. king of Prussia who was proclaimed German emperor

f. leader of the Young Italy movement

g. emperor of Austria and king of Hungary

h. legislative assembly, or the lower house of the German legislature

i. chief minister of Sardinia

j. nomadic warriors living in Hungary who were opposed to Austrian rule

FILL IN THE BLANK (*3 points each*) Choose from the following list to complete each of the statements below.

Treaty of San Stefano   pogroms   Emancipation Edict
risorgimento   People's Will   Balkan League
Kulturkampf   kaiser   Junkers
Carbonari

1. The Italian word for resurgence, _____, became the name for the nationalist movement in Italy.

2. The _____ was the name of a secret nationalist group working for the liberation and unification of Italy.

3. The German emperor, or _____, held great power under the constitution that united the 25 German states.

4. Wealthy German landowners, called _____, worked to reduce trade restrictions between German states.

5. The program of _____ was a series of anti-Catholic laws passed to weaken the church's influence in Germany.

6. Czar Alexander II's _____ essentially ended the practice of serfdom in Russia.

7. A group called the _____ used methods of terrorism, such as assassinations and bombings, to try to get their demands met.

8. More than 100 Jewish towns were destroyed in riots called

_____ as minority discrimination increased in the late 1800s.

9. The _____ ended a war between the Turks and the Russians and granted independence to Romania, Serbia, and Montenegro.

10. Bulgaria, Serbia, Greece, and Montenegro became known as the

_____ .

TRUE/FALSE *(2 points each)* Mark each statement *T* if it is true or *F* if it is false.

_____ **1.** Even after unification, tension still existed between northern and southern Italy.

_____ **2.** Giuseppe Garibaldi and more than 1,000 soldiers defeated King Victor Emmanuel II and gained control of Sardinia.

_____ **3.** The German Social Democratic party was able to gain control of the Reichstag and overturn many laws passed by the Bundesrat.

_____ **4.** The three different regions of Russia were united by a common language, customs, and economic system.

_____ **5.** The Dual Monarchy was a good arrangement for Austria and Hungary because each region produced something the other needed.

Chapter 25, Chapter Test Form C, continued

IDENTIFICATION *(3 points each)* Identify to which country the following terms are most related and place the letter of that term under the appropriate country.

 a. Duma

 b. Lajos Kossuth

 c. Social Democratic Party

 d. Sardinia

 e. Zollverein

 f. *zemstvos*

 g. Prussia

 h. nihilists

 i. Expedition of the Thousand

 j. Serbia

ITALY	GERMANY	RUSSIA	AUSTRIA-HUNGARY
_____	_____	_____	_____
_____	_____	_____	_____
	_____	_____	

Modern Chapter **17**

Chapter Test Form C
The Age of Imperialism

MATCHING *(3 points each)* Place the letters of the descriptions next to the appropriate names and terms.

_____ **1.** imperialism

_____ **2.** protectorate

_____ **3.** al-Mahdī

_____ **4.** Cecil Rhodes

_____ **5.** Shaka

_____ **6.** paternalism

_____ **7.** Mongkut

_____ **8.** Liliuokalani

_____ **9.** Porfirio Díaz

_____ **10.** Carlos Juan Finlay

a. when one country takes control of another country

b. Zulu leader who created an empire with a strong army

c. an area or country where local leaders keep their titles, but actual control comes from the outside

d. king of Siam who studied Western ideas

e. Mexican dictator

f. governing a colony in the same way parents guide their children

g. British businessman who controlled South African diamond production

h. Cuban doctor who discovered that mosquitoes carry yellow fever

i. first woman ever to rule the Hawaiian Islands

j. led a revolt against Egyptian rule

FILL IN THE BLANK *(2 points each)* Choose from the following list to complete each of the statements below.

buffer state   Fashoda crisis   assimilation
Meiji Restoration   Sino-Japanese War

1. France and Great Britain both struggled to gain control of a portion of the upper

Nile during the _____.

2. Africans were not willing to give up their culture and adopt the European culture, so

they often fought against _____.

3. A group of Japanese samurai returned the emperor to power in the

_____.

4. A Korean rebellion led to the _____.

5. Siam served as a _____ between British-controlled Burma and French Indochina.

Chapter 26, Chapter Test Form C, continued

TRUE/FALSE *(3 points each)* Mark each statement *T* if it is true or *F* if it is false.

_____ **1.** Major European governments planned their imperialism carefully.

_____ **2.** An increase in industrialization led to an increase in imperialism because of the greater need for raw materials and markets for new products.

_____ **3.** When Tunis was a French protectorate, the Turkish governor actually controlled the country.

_____ **4.** Many European countries were interested in controlling Morocco because of its location on the Strait of Gibraltar.

_____ **5.** The British gained control of the Suez Canal by defeating the Egyptians in battle.

_____ **6.** Due to their superior military strength, European countries had little problem colonizing Africa.

_____ **7.** Descendents of Dutch settlers left Cape Colony and moved north and east after the British took control of the colony.

_____ **8.** Some Indian nationalists wanted to break all ties with Great Britain quickly, while others wanted to gain independence slowly.

_____ **9.** Fear of imperialists in Asia caused the Japanese to avoid colonizing other countries.

_____ **10.** Europeans and Americans gained control of Latin American economies by investing money in different businesses.

ORGANIZATION *(3 points each)* Complete the chart below by writing the letter of each name or term in the correct box.

a. Emilio Aguinaldo

b. Panama Canal

c. Boer War

d. Guam

e. Suez Canal

f. Samory Touré

g. Sino-Japanese War

h. Spanish-American War

i. Taiwan

j. Venustiano Carranza

	AFRICA	ASIA	PACIFIC ISLANDS	LATIN AMERICA
IMPORTANT PLACES				
REBEL LEADERS		✕		
WARS OR CONFLICTS			✕	

UNIT **6**   Unit Test Form C

Modern Unit **4**   **Industrialization and Nationalism**

MATCHING *(2 points each)* Place the letters of the descriptions next to the appropriate terms.

_____ **1.** imperialism

_____ **2.** protectorate

_____ **3.** assimilation

_____ **4.** autocrat

_____ **5.** kaiser

_____ **6.** pogroms

_____ **7.** suffrage

_____ **8.** anarchists

_____ **9.** sectionalism

_____ **10.** romanticism

_____ **11.** emigration

_____ **12.** suburbs

_____ **13.** vulcanization

_____ **14.** mechanization

_____ **15.** interchangeable parts

a. invention that led to the use of an assembly line to mass produce an item

b. residential areas on the outskirts of a city that form as a city grows

c. the movement of people away from their native lands

d. the right to vote

e. a leader holding absolute power

f. one country forcibly taking control of another country's government, trade, or culture

g. the process of giving up one's own culture to adopt the culture of another group

h. an area where local leaders keep their titles, but are controlled by outside powers

i. title given to the German emperor

j. Russian riots that resulted in the massacre of many Jews

k. competition among regions of a country

l. people who oppose all formal government

m. an artistic movement that valued emotions and instinct above reason

n. the use of machines to increase the amount of material produced

o. process used to make rubber less sticky, and practical to work with

FILL IN THE BLANK *(3 points each)* Choose from the following list to complete each of the statements below.

Jane Addams	Fashoda crisis	Thomas Edison
social Darwinism	Emancipation Edict	J.P. Morgan
Florence Nightingale	Karl Marx	

1. _____ is credited with creating the modern profession of nursing, by establishing professional training and a school for nurses during the Crimean War.

2. _____ founded the United States Steel Company, one of the first billion-dollar corporations in America.

3. The practice of serfdom was ended by Czar Alexander II's

_____.

4. _____ created a model for community service centers when she opened Hull House, a home for the poor.

5. A system of transmitting electricity from a central powerhouse to other places was

developed by _____.

6. _____ is the belief that the wealthy succeed because they possess abilities that are superior to the abilities of the poor.

7. The Communist Manifesto was published by Frederich Engles and

_____, who believed that utopian socialism was impractical.

8. The struggle between Great Britain and France to gain control of the upper Nile is

known as the _____.

TRUE/FALSE *(2 points each)* Mark each statement *T* if it is true or *F* if it is false.

_____ **1.** Individuals own and operate businesses under an economic system called socialism.

_____ **2.** Scientists were able to trace malaria and yellow fever to germs carried in mosquitoes.

_____ **3.** Petroleum is crude oil used to power ships, cars, and airplanes.

_____ **4.** The United States was strengthened by sectionalism.

_____ **5.** A common language, common customs, and a unified economic system united Russia's three regions.

_____ **6.** The Carbonari was the name of a secret nationalist group working for the liberation and unification of Italy.

_____ **7.** Morocco was desired by many European countries because of its location on the Strait of Gibraltar.

_____ **8.** The United States gained permanent control of Cuba after the Spanish-American War.

Unit 6, Unit Test Form C, continued

IDENTIFICATION *(3 points each)* Fill in the chart below by determining which country is associated with each leader, event, or movement.

a. Boer War

b. Catholic Emancipation Act

c. Social Democratic Labor Party

d. the Duma

e. Northwest Ordinance

f. Samory Touré

g. Benjamin Disraeli

h. Alexander II

i. Abraham Lincoln

j. Chartist movement

United States	Russia	Africa	Great Britain
_____	_____	_____	_____
_____	_____	_____	_____
	_____		_____

CHAPTER 27

Modern Chapter 18

Chapter Test Form C

World War I and the Russian Revolution

MATCHING *(3 points each)* Place the letters of the descriptions next to the appropriate names and terms.

_____ **1.** Triple Alliance

_____ **2.** Triple Entente

_____ **3.** Francis Ferdinand

_____ **4.** Manfred von Richthofen

_____ **5.** armistice

_____ **6.** propaganda

_____ **7.** Woodrow Wilson

_____ **8.** genocide

_____ **9.** economic sanctions

_____ **10.** mandate

a. "The Red Baron," a famous German pilot

b. information, both true and false, meant to get people to back their country's war efforts

c. alliance between Germany, Italy, and Austria-Hungary

d. one type of penalty that the League of Nations could impose on a country

e. American president during World War I

f. heir to the Austro-Hungarian throne, whose assassination contributed to the start of the war

g. a colony that is ruled by an "advanced" nation until the colony is considered ready for independence

h. alliance between France, Great Britain, and Russia

i. systematic extermination of an ethnic group

j. an agreement to stop fighting

FILL IN THE BLANK *(3 points each)* Choose from the following list to complete each of the statements below.

Big Four	Fourteen Points	ultimatum
Bolshevik	League of Nations	belligerents
militarism	total war	

1. Prior to World War I, European leaders believed that _____, or threat of force, would help them achieve their goals.

2. The _____ sent by Austria-Hungary to the Serbian government demanded their complete support of the Austro-Hungarian government.

3. Belgium, a neutral country, agreed not to help any _____, or warring nations.

4. World War I was known as a "_____," because the nations involved turned all of their resources to the war effort.

Chapter 27, Chapter Test Form C, continued

5. The ideals of the radical _____ faction appealed to war-weary and hungry Russian people.

6. Woodrow Wilson set forth a plan, known as the _____, meant to contribute to a more peaceful, just world after the end of the war.

7. The chief negotiators of the Paris Peace Conference were called the

_____.

8. The Treaty of Versailles provided for the formation of a world organization to

maintain peace, known as the _____.

TRUE/FALSE *(2 points each)* Mark each statement *T* if it is true or *F* if it is false.

_____ **1.** Germany formed an alliance with Russia in order to prevent an alliance between Russia and France.

_____ **2.** Great Britain declared war on Germany when Germany sent soldiers to Belgium.

_____ **3.** The Ottoman Empire was an important ally to the Germans because of their control of the Dardanelles.

_____ **4.** Woodrow Wilson's ideas for a peace treaty that was fair to all were fully supported by the other negotiators.

_____ **5.** The Russians had a small army, but they were well-equipped and had plenty of resources.

_____ **6.** Vladimir Lenin was a leader of the Menshevik faction.

_____ **7.** The Communist Party overthrew the government of Russia and signed a peace treaty with the Central Powers, ending their part in World War I.

_____ **8.** The leaders of the Central Powers controlled negotiations during the Paris Peace Conference.

IDENTIFICATION *(3 points each)* Determine whether each term or name is associated with the Central Powers or the Allied Powers. Write the letter of each correct answer in the appropriate column on the chart.

a. defeated at the Battle of Tannenberg

b. France

c. sank the *Lusitania*

d. Arthur Zimmermann

e. Great Britain

f. Austria-Hungary

g. withdrew from Gallipoli

h. Germany

i. introduced poison gas as a weapon

j. Ferdinand Foch

Central Powers	Allied Powers
_____	_____
_____	_____
_____	_____
_____	_____
_____	_____

CHAPTER **28**

Modern Chapter **19**

Chapter Test Form C

The Great Depression and the Rise of Totalitarianism

MATCHING *(3 points each)* Place the letters of the descriptions next to the appropriate names and terms.

_____ **1.** Joseph Stalin

_____ **2.** Adolf Hitler

_____ **3.** James Joyce

_____ **4.** economic nationalism

_____ **5.** Sinn Fein

_____ **6.** Ramsay MacDonald

_____ **7.** Salvador Dali

_____ **8.** Great Depression

_____ **9.** Frank Lloyd Wright

_____ **10.** Maginot Line

a. Irish author who used the "stream of consciousness" technique in his book, *Ulysses*

b. when prices and wages fell and unemployment rose, all in a very brief period of time

c. Spanish surrealist artist

d. fortifications along France's border with Germany, to prevent German invasion

e. British leader of the Labour Party who formed a coalition government

f. Irish nationalist party that led the Irish Republican Army

g. policy that tries to protect domestic industries by limiting trade with other countries

h. leader of the Nazi party who, once in power, called himself *der Führer*

i. led the Communist Party in Russia

j. architect with the new idea that a building should fit into its environment

FILL IN THE BLANK *(3 points each)* Choose from the following list to complete each of the statements below.

Rome-Berlin Axis	cubism	command economy
Black Tuesday	New Deal	Black Shirts
market speculations	Easter Rising	purge
influenza pandemic		

1. A geometric art form called _____ was influenced by traditional African art and often showed objects from several viewpoints at once.

2. A mysterious and terrifying outbreak of disease, known as the

_____, spread throughout the world during World War I.

3. Risky investments known as _____ were a cause of the stock market crash of 1929.

Chapter 28, Chapter Test Form C, continued

4. The U.S. government's plan to provide relief and reform to the American economic

system was known as the _____.

5. Stalin led a _____, or large-scale elimination, killing party
members and others who were thought to be disloyal to him.

6. The alliance between Hitler and Mussolini was called the

_____.

7. Investors on the New York Stock Exchange rushed to sell their overvalued stocks,

causing widespread panic on a day known as _____.

8. The British put down the _____, a bloody revolt by Irish
nationalists, and executed many of its leaders.

9. The _____ were Fascists who claimed that their purpose was
to defend Italy against a communist revolution.

10. In a _____, the government controls all economic decisions.

TRUE/FALSE *(2 points each)* Mark each statement *T* if it is true or *F* if it is false.

_____ **1.** Literature and art after World War I demonstrated feelings of being
disconnected from society by breaking from traditional forms and subjects.

_____ **2.** The ability to buy items on credit contributed to people focusing on the
present moment instead of planning for the future.

_____ **3.** The United States escaped the economic devastation that affected many
countries after the war.

_____ **4.** The Social Security Act of 1935 provided for unemployment and old-age
benefits.

_____ **5.** After the war, nearly one-quarter of Great Britain's population was
unemployed.

_____ **6.** Catholics and Protestants in Ireland joined forces after the war.

_____ **7.** Communism was popular with workers because it promised to eliminate
social classes and share all property.

_____ **8.** The Nazi Party is also known as the National Socialist German Workers'
Party.

IDENTIFICATION *(3 points each)* Match each political leader and term with the appropriate country. Write the letters in the correct columns on the chart.

a. Joseph Stalin

b. Benito Mussolini

c. Adolf Hitler

d. Léon Blum

e. Fascist Party

f. Politburo

g. Popular Front

h. Third Reich

France	Germany	Russia	Italy
_____	_____	_____	_____
_____	_____	_____	_____

CHAPTER 29

Chapter Test Form C

Modern Chapter 20 **Nationalist Movements Around the World**

MATCHING *(2 points each)* Place the letters of the descriptions next to the appropriate names and terms.

_____ **1.** Mohandas Gandhi

_____ **2.** Reza Shah Pahlavi

_____ **3.** Mao Zedong

_____ **4.** Sun Yixian

_____ **5.** Rafael Trujillo Molina

_____ **6.** Léopold Senghor

_____ **7.** Chiang Kai-shek

_____ **8.** Fulgencio Batista

a. leader of Persia who officially changed Persia's name to Iran

b. dictator of the Dominican Republic

c. director of the Chinese Nationalist Party

d. leader of the Indian nationalist movement who preached nonviolent civil disobedience

e. believed that Chinese peasants were the key to a communist revolution in China

f. leader of an African anti-colonial movement

g. army sergeant who had American support in overthrowing the Cuban government

h. strengthened the Nationalist army in order to stop Chinese warlord resistance

FILL IN THE BLANK *(3 points each)* Choose from the following list to complete each of the statements below.

militarism   Balfour Declaration   Treaty of Portsmouth
nitrates   Wafd Party   Kuomintang
Boxer Rebellion   passive resistance   Open Door Policy
Good Neighbor Policy

1. After World War I, the Egyptian _____ led a nationalist movement against the British.

2. The _____ proclaimed Britain's support for a Jewish homeland in Palestine.

3. Nonviolent civil disobedience is called _____.

4. The U.S. government asked other nations to recognize their

_____, which would allow all nations equal access to trade with China.

5. The _____ was a major anti-foreigner movement that swept through China at the end of the 1800s.

6. The _____, or the Chinese Nationalist Party, believed that China could protect itself against foreign control if it became a modern nation.

7. The _____ ended the Russo-Japanese War.

8. The attitudes of a nation influenced by _____ are shaped by military needs, values, and goals.

9. With President Roosevelt's _____, the United States pledged noninterference in Latin American affairs.

10. Chile's chief export was _____, which are used in fertilizers and explosives.

TRUE/FALSE *(3 points each)* Mark each statement *T* if it is true or *F* if it is false.

_____ **1.** Egypt was Great Britain's largest colony.

_____ **2.** Mustafa Kemal worked to westernize Turkey.

_____ **3.** Africans preferred life as a British colony, and had little interest in independence.

_____ **4.** Troops from Great Britain, France, Germany, Russia, Japan, and the United States went to China to end the Boxer Rebellion and protect their interests in the country.

_____ **5.** The Empress Dowager Tz'u-hsi was enthusiastic about the modernization of China.

_____ **6.** Japan created an alliance with Great Britain because of the threat posed by the Chinese Communist Party.

_____ **7.** The abundance of raw materials in Japan made modernization easy.

_____ **8.** Agricultural products were the primary export of Latin America.

_____ **9.** Diego Rivera was a military leader who overthrew Mexico's elected government.

_____ **10.** Latin American labor unions used strikes to improve working conditions.

Chapter 29, Chapter Test Form C, continued

ORGANIZATION *(3 points each)* Complete the chart by matching each name or phrase with the correct nation. Write the letter of each name or phrase in the appropriate column.

a. Long March

b. Arthur Balfour

c. Zionism

d. British military controls Suez Canal

e. Wafd Party

f. British allow the people to elect representatives

g. Three Principles of the People

h. Mohandas Gandhi

Egypt	Middle East	India	China
_____	_____	_____	_____
_____	_____	_____	_____

CHAPTER 30   Chapter Test Form C

Modern Chapter **21**   **World War II**

MATCHING *(3 points each)* Place the letters of the descriptions next to the appropriate terms.

_____ **1.** appeasement

_____ **2.** Luftwaffe

_____ **3.** Auschwitz

_____ **4.** isolationists

_____ **5.** Neutrality Acts

_____ **6.** Lend-Lease Act

_____ **7.** blitzkrieg

_____ **8.** Kellogg-Briand Pact

_____ **9.** maquis

_____ **10.** collaborators

a. agreement between more than 60 nations making war "illegal"

b. policy in which the demands of the aggressor are met in order to keep peace

c. type of warfare involving attacks of great speed and force

d. people willing to work against their country to help the enemy

e. name given to French underground resistance movements that worked against Germany

f. Hitler's air force

g. Americans who believed the United States should stay out of World War II

h. prevented the United States from selling war equipment to warring nations

i. a Nazi concentration camp

j. authorized the U.S. president to supply Britain with war materials on credit

FILL IN THE BLANK *(2 points each)* Choose from the following list to complete each of the statements below.

V-E Day	V-J Day	Anti-Comintern Pact
Francisco Franco	Winston Churchill	Bataan Death March
Heinrich Himmler	Charles de Gaulle	

1. _____ led the Nationalists in the Spanish Civil War.

2. Germany and Japan signed the _____, in which they pledged to stop communism.

3. _____ was considered to be one of the greatest leaders in Britain.

4. General _____ led the the Free French government from London while France was occupied by the Germans.

5. _____ was the day victory over the Axis Powers was declared in Europe.

6. The head of the SS, _____, led Hitler's Final Solution in an attempt to eliminate Jews.

7. The Japanese surrendered to the Allies on _____, September 2, 1945.

8. The _____, which covered 55 miles and was forced upon 78,000 prisoners, resulted in the deaths of 600 Americans and as many as 10,000 Filipinos.

TRUE/FALSE *(3 points each)* Mark each statement *T* if it is true or *F* if it is false.

_____ **1.** The League of Nations provided military protection to Ethiopia against Italy.

_____ **2.** The army, the landowners, and the Roman Catholic Church all held positions of power under the rule of Francisco Franco.

_____ **3.** Germany and the Soviet Union signed a pact agreeing to never attack each other.

_____ **4.** The Germans, the Italians, and the French reached a fair agreement that secured peace between them.

_____ **5.** The Battle of Britain lasted only seven days.

_____ **6.** The United States was eager to enter World War II in order to protect its European allies.

_____ **7.** Hitler planned to eliminate the Jews in his quest for the perfect "Aryan race."

_____ **8.** Anne Frank died in a Nazi concentration camp.

_____ **9.** During the Holocaust, the Nazis killed six million European Jews.

_____ **10.** The use of the atomic bomb by the United States led to the surrender of Japan.

Chapter 30, Chapter Test Form C, continued

IDENTIFICATION *(3 points each)* Match each cause with the resulting effect. Write the letters in the appropriate spaces in the chart.

  a. Battle of Stalingrad

  b. Hitler is allowed to annex Sudetenland, and takes over Czechoslovakia

  c. the Japanese bomb Pearl Harbor

  d. German forces attack Poland

  e. France is taken back, and Germany surrenders

  f. Allied troops land on D-Day on France's Normandy coast

  g. World War II begins

  h. the Allies attack "the soft underbelly of the Axis"

  i. German forces are defeated and never fully recover

  j. Munich Conference

  k. Mussolini is forced to resign

  l. United States enters World War II

Cause	Effect

UNIT 7

Modern Unit **5**

Unit Test Form C

World War in the Twentieth Century

MATCHING *(3 points each)* Place the letters of the descriptions next to the appropriate names and terms.

_____ **1.** Winston Churchill

_____ **2.** Charles de Gaulle

_____ **3.** Mao Zedong

_____ **4.** Joseph Stalin

_____ **5.** Adolf Hitler

_____ **6.** Benito Mussolini

_____ **7.** Franklin D. Roosevelt

_____ **8.** Manfred von Richthofen

_____ **9.** Woodrow Wilson

_____ **10.** Fulgencio Batista

a. "The Red Baron," a famous German pilot

b. army sergeant who had American support in overthrowing the Cuban government

c. considered one of the greatest British leaders

d. French general who led the Free French government during World War II

e. American president who entered World War I

f. led the Communist Party in Russia

g. leader of the Chinese Communist Party

h. facist dictator who formed the Rome-Berlin Axis with Hitler

i. American president who introduced the "New Deal"

j. leader of the Nazi party

FILL IN THE BLANK *(3 points each)* Choose from the following list to complete each of the statements below.

total war   command economy   passive resistance
economic sanctions   market speculations   appeasement
armistice   nitrates   blitzkrieg
isolationists

1. _____, which are used in fertilizers and explosives, were Chile's chief export.

2. Risky investments, known as _____, were a cause of the U.S. stock market crash.

3. The Nazi's introduced _____, a type of warfare involving fast, forceful attacks.

4. Those in the United States who wished to stay out of World War II were called

_____.

5. In 1918, a German delegation signed an _____, or agreement to stop fighting, that ended World War I.

6. World War I was known as a "_____," because the nations involved turned all of their resources to the war effort.

7. Mohandas Gandhi taught _____, or nonviolent civil disobedience.

8. In a _____, the government controls all economic decisions.

9. At the Munich Conference, Hitler was given an _____, allowing him to have some of his demands met in an attempt to maintain peace.

10. The League of Nations could impose _____, or trade blocks, on a country who did not cooperate.

TRUE/FALSE *(2 points each)* Mark each statement *T* if it is true or *F* if it is false.

_____ **1.** The Nazis practiced genocide.

_____ **2.** The League of Nations was a result of the Treaty of Versailles.

_____ **3.** The arts were generally unaffected by World War I.

_____ **4.** The working class generally opposes communism because of its elitist beliefs.

_____ **5.** The Boxer Rebellion was one of the anti-foreigner movements that swept through China at the end of the 1800s.

_____ **6.** The Treaty of Portsmouth ended World War II.

_____ **7.** Agricultural products were the primary export of Latin America.

_____ **8.** The Japanese surrendered on V-E Day.

_____ **9.** Auschwitz was one of the Nazi concentration camps in which many Jews were killed.

_____ **10.** Japan surrendered, ending World War II, shortly after the United States dropped two atomic bombs on their country.

Unit 7, Unit Test Form C, continued

IDENTIFICATION *(3 points each)* Match each name or phrase to the world war with which it is associated. Write each letter in the correct place on the chart.

a. D-Day

b. Pearl Harbor

c. first use of U-boats

d. Treaty of Versailles

e. Central Powers

f. Battle of Britain

g. atomic bomb

h. Woodrow Wilson

i. Austria-Hungary

j. Adolf Hitler

World War I	World War II
_____	_____
_____	_____
_____	_____
_____	_____
_____	_____

CHAPTER 31   Chapter Test Form C

Modern Chapter **22**   **Europe and North America in the Postwar Years**

MATCHING *(3 points each)* Place the letters of the descriptions next to the appropriate terms.

_____ **1.** NAACP

_____ **2.** Warsaw Pact

_____ **3.** Lyndon Johnson

_____ **4.** Martin Luther King Jr.

_____ **5.** United Nations

_____ **6.** Truman Doctrine

_____ **7.** Nikita Khrushchev

_____ **8.** Cominform

_____ **9.** Marshall Plan

_____ **10.** Joseph McCarthy

a. organization of nations designed to keep international peace and solve problems

b. policy declaring communism a threat to democracy and calling for the United States to support free peoples

c. program that provided massive economic relief to many European nations

d. organization of European communist parties designed to oppose U.S. relief efforts

e. alliance of Eastern bloc nations that adopted a 20-year mutual defense agreement

f. successor of Stalin who lifted many of Stalin's restrictions on the Soviet people

g. U.S. senator who wrongly accused many people of being communists

h. developed a program called the Great Society

i. civil rights organization for African Americans

j. well-known civil rights leader who was assassinated in 1968

FILL IN THE BLANK *(3 points each)* Choose from the following list to complete each of the statements below.

containment	Security Council	Cold War
welfare state	Berlin Airlift	Cuban missile crisis
Nürnberg trials	veto power	

1. An international court held the _____ to try Nazi leaders accused of war crimes.

2. One branch of the UN, known as the _____, includes ten temporary members and five permanent member nations.

3. _____ is the ability to defeat a measure with a single vote.

4. The _____ was a struggle of ideas and worldviews between communism and democracy.

5. The _____ was probably the most dangerous moment of the Cold War.

6. The term _____ was used to describe the U.S. policy of restricting the spread of communism.

7. The _____ was so successful that it even allowed for raw materials to be supplied to factories.

8. In a _____, the government takes primary responsibility for the social welfare of its citizens.

TRUE/FALSE *(2 points each)* Mark each statement *T* if it is true or *F* if it is false.

_____ 1. The Soviet Union and the Western Allies developed a unified plan for postwar Europe.

_____ 2. The Truman Doctrine stated that the United States would not try to stamp out communism in countries where it already existed.

_____ 3. The Warsaw Pact troops greatly outnumbered the NATO troops in Europe.

_____ 4. The United States and other Western powers used nuclear weapons as a deterrent.

_____ 5. West Germany followed a free-market policy.

_____ 6. The Deutsche mark was a powerful unit of currency used in the Soviet Union.

_____ 7. Charles de Gaulle played an important role in the recovery of postwar France.

_____ 8. The only real Soviet innovations were in military and space technology.

IDENTIFICATION *(6 points each)* Place the following events leading to the Cold War in the order in which they occurred.

a. Soviets and their allies became known as the Eastern bloc, and the United States was supported by Western democracies and other noncommunist countries.

b. Because of a conflict in peace talks, Germany was divided into eastern and western parts.

c. Disagreements occurred over the occupation of postwar Germany.

d. Stalin's view of free elections differed from Western ideas.

e. The Allied powers' alliance dissolved.

1. _____

2. _____

3. _____

4. _____

5. _____

Chapter Test Form C

Asia Since 1945

MATCHING (*3 points each*) Place the letters of the descriptions next to the appropriate terms.

_____ **1.** Jawaharlal Nehru

_____ **2.** Benazir Bhutto

_____ **3.** Gang of Four

_____ **4.** Red Guards

_____ **5.** Ferdinand Marcos

_____ **6.** Corazon Aquino

_____ **7.** Ho Chi Minh

_____ **8.** Khmer Rouge

_____ **9.** Aung San Suu Kyi

_____ **10.** Pol Pot

a. the first woman to lead a Muslim nation

b. widow of an assassinated political leader who became leader of the Phillipines

c. group formed by Jiang Qing to continue China's Cultural Revolution

d. leader of Viet Minh, against whom the United States fought in the Vietnam War

e. India's first prime minister

f. won the Nobel Peace Prize for her work in Burma

g. corrupt Philippine president supported by the United States

h. radical student group chosen to lead China's Cultural Revolution

i. leader of the corrupt communist Cambodian government

j. group of Cambodian Communists responsible for over 1 million Cambodian deaths

FILL IN THE BLANK (*3 points each*) Choose from the following list to complete each of the statements below.

Great Leap Forward	Cultural Revolution	MacArthur Constitution
zaibatsu	Muslim League	Geneva Accord
ASEAN	Four Tigers	mixed economy
"Quit India"		

1. A group of Indian Muslims called the _____ rejected Sir Stafford Cripps' plan for Indian independence.

2. After participating in Mohandas Gandhi's _____ campaign, Gandhi and 60,000 of his followers were arrested.

Chapter 32, Chapter Test Form C, continued

3. India had a _____, meaning some of its businesses were privately owned while the rest were owned by the government.

4. The Chinese plan to improve industrial output, called the

   _____, was a failure—industrial production actually decreased.

5. Mao Zedong tried to redefine people's customs, habits, and thoughts through a

   _____.

6. The _____ set up a democratic, nonmilitary government in Japan.

7. Some of the _____, or family–owned conglomerates, were broken up in order to encourage Japanese free trade.

8. The war between the French and Viet Minh ended with the signing of the

   _____.

9. Southeast Asian countries formed _____ to promote economic growth and regional security.

10. South Korea, Taiwan, Singapore, and Hong Kong became known as the

    _____, because of their strong economies.

TRUE/FALSE *(2 points each)* Mark each statement *T* if it is true or *F* if it is false.

_____ 1. India's first constitution after independence called for an elected president and parliament.

_____ 2. The Awami League was a militant group that wanted to take over the government of India.

_____ 3. After World War II, the Communist party defeated the Nationalists and gained control of China.

_____ 4. Deng Xiaoping instituted a plan called the Four Modernizations, designed to reform China's economy.

_____ 5. The events in Tiananmen Square helped improve China's relations with the West.

Chapter 32, Chapter Test Form C, continued

IDENTIFICATION *(2 points each)* Match each word or phrase with the country it was most associated with after World War II. Write the letter of each name or term in the appropriate column on the chart.

a. Muhammad Ali Jinnah

b. zaibatsu

c. 38th parallel

d. LDP

e. Jiang Qing

f. Red Guards

g. Kim Il Sung

h. Paris Peace Accords

i. Muslim League

j. Kim Dae Jung

k. SCAP

l. Tet Offensive

m. Rajiv Gandhi

n. 17th parallel

o. Tiananmen Square Massacre

India	China	Korea	Vietnam	Japan
_____	_____	_____	_____	_____
_____	_____	_____	_____	_____
_____	_____	_____	_____	_____

CHAPTER 33   Chapter Test Form C

Modern Chapter 24   **Africa and the Middle East Since 1945**

MATCHING *(2 points each)* Place the letters of the descriptions next to the appropriate terms.

_____ **1.** Kwame Nkrumah

_____ **2.** Charles de Gaulle

_____ **3.** Nelson Mandela

_____ **4.** Ba'ath Party

_____ **5.** OPEC

_____ **6.** Tehran

_____ **7.** CIA

_____ **8.** Yasir Arafat

a. first elected president of South Africa

b. dictatorial party which was originally Pan-Arab

c. leader of the Palestine Liberation Organization

d. leader of the Ghana revolutionary movement

e. international organization of oil producing countries

f. French president

g. site where Iranians held the U.S. embassy hostage

h. U.S. agency that engineered a coup in Iran to put a dictator into power

FILL IN THE BLANK *(3 points each)* Choose from the following list to complete each of the statements below.

Kikuyu	intifada	apartheid
Suez Crisis	Six-Day War	Pan–African Movement
kibbutz	petrodollars	

1. The _____ was a worldwide effort seeking equality for black people.

2. The _____, Kenya's largest ethnic group, struggled for Kenyan independence.

3. A South African policy known as _____ called for the segregation of races.

4. As the Jewish population of Israel increased, the collective farm, or

_____, helped turn desert areas into usable farmland.

5. During the _____, Egypt fought against Israel, Britain, and France.

6. Israel captured the Sinai Peninsula, the Gaza Strip, the West Bank, and East

Jerusalem during the _____.

Chapter 33, Chapter Test Form C, continued

7. Palestinians revolted against Israeli occupation in uprisings called

_____.

8. Oil profits, or _____, paid for economic development throughout the Persian Gulf area.

TRUE/FALSE *(3 points each)* Mark each statement *T* if it is true or *F* if it is false.

_____ **1.** Civil disobedience, strikes, and riots helped the people of Ghana win their independence.

_____ **2.** The Mau Mau used nonviolent means to gain Kenyan independence.

_____ **3.** French leaders used military might to force their African colonies to become part of the French Community.

_____ **4.** Belgium did not want to lose control of the Congo because it depended on the colony's natural resources.

_____ **5.** Dictatorships often followed the independence of African colonies because the military stepped in to keep peace when living conditions did not improve fast enough.

_____ **6.** In Algeria, Europeans known as *colons* made up 90 percent of the country's population.

_____ **7.** The Camp David Accords led to a peace treaty between Egypt and Israel.

_____ **8.** OPEC sets world oil prices and production levels.

_____ **9.** The Ayatollah Khomeini worked to establish a monarchy in Iran.

_____ **10.** Saddam Hussein and the Ba'ath Party took control of Iran in 1968.

Chapter 33, Chapter Test Form C, continued

IDENTIFICATION *(3 points each)* Use the list below to fill in the chart. Write the letter of each country, name, or year in the appropriate box.

a. Kwame Nkrumah

b. Great Britain

c. 1963

d. Sékou Touré

e. France

f. 1960

g. Patrice Lumumba

h. Belgium

i. Jomo Kenyatta

j. 1957

	Ghana	Guinea	Congo	Kenya
The colony's founding country	**1.**	**4.**	**6.**	Great Britain
Nationalist movement leader	**2.**	**5.**	**7.**	**9.**
Year of independence	**3.**	1958	**8.**	**10.**

CHAPTER  **34**

Modern Chapter 25

Chapter Test Form C

Latin America Since 1945

MATCHING *(2 points each)* Place the letters of the descriptions next to the appropriate names.

_____ **1.** Carlos Salinas de Gortari

_____ **2.** Daniel Ortega

_____ **3.** Oscar Arias

_____ **4.** Fidel Castro

_____ **5.** Eva Perón

a. leader of the Sandinistas

b. leader of the Cuban revolution

c. Mexican president

d. considered the hero of the working class in Argentina

e. president of Costa Rica

FILL IN THE BLANK *(3 points each)* Choose from the following list to complete each of the statements below.

dirty war	monoculture	multinational corporations
Contadora Principles	Falkland Islands	"Brazilian Miracle"
Grenada	contras	inflation
dissidents		

1. Many _____ were encouraged to do business in Latin America in order to increase industrialization.

2. Overdependence on one or two natural resources, or _____, led to economic instability in Latin America.

3. As governments print more money to pay off their debts, the value of that money decreases, causing _____.

4. A rebel group, called the _____, received U.S. support to overthrow the Nicaraguan government.

5. The _____ was a document signed by Colombia, Mexico, Panama, and Venezuela.

6. Many Cuban _____ disagreed with the government and sought political asylum in other countries.

Chapter 34, Chapter Test Form C, continued

7. U.S. troops restored a democratic government to _____.

8. The _____ brought economic gain at the cost of civil rights.

9. The Argentinean government's attempt to eliminate its opponents became known as

the _____.

10. The British defeated the Argentinean military and maintained control of the

_____.

TRUE/FALSE *(3 points each)* Mark each statement *T* if it is true or *F* if it is false.

_____ **1.** Latin American countries placed heavy tariffs on foreign goods and supported domestic production with a policy known as import substitution.

_____ **2.** Latin American countries developed large amounts of debt by borrowing the money necessary for industrialization.

_____ **3.** Rapid industrialization in Latin America led to a high standard of living and very low poverty rates.

_____ **4.** Vincente Fox was elected president of Mexico in 2000, the first non-PRI president in more than 70 years.

_____ **5.** The United States invaded Panama to take control of the Panama Canal.

_____ **6.** Rebels, supported by the United States, landed at the Bay of Pigs and overthrew the Cuban dictatorship.

_____ **7.** François Duvalier and his son, Jean-Claude, improved economic conditions in Haiti.

_____ **8.** Jean-Bertrand Aristide was elected in 1990, becoming the first democratically elected leader of Haiti.

_____ **9.** The Shining Path fought to bring democracy to Peru.

_____ **10.** Augusto Pinochet led a coup against the Colombian government.

Chapter 34, Chapter Test Form C, continued

IDENTIFICATION *(6 points each)* Compare and contrast the difficulties Mexico and Brazil had following World War II. Write the letter of each word or phrase in the appropriate space on the diagram.

- **a.** earthquake
- **b.** debt
- **c.** inflation
- **d.** Chiapas peasant uprising
- **e.** unemployment
- **f.** slumping oil prices
- **g.** banned political parties
- **h.** population explosion
- **i.** loss of civil rights
- **j.** military government

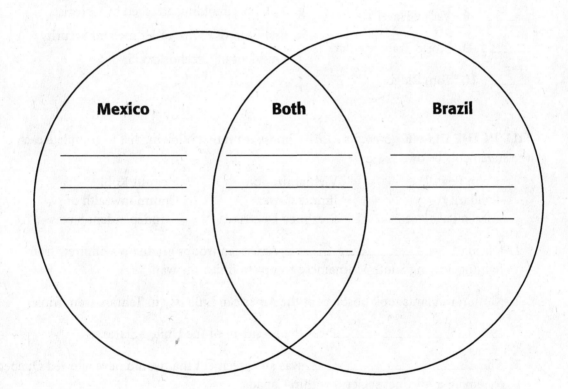

CHAPTER  35

Modern Chapter **26**

Chapter Test Form C

The Superpowers in the Modern Era

MATCHING *(3 points each)* Place the letters of the descriptions next to the appropriate terms.

_____ **1.** détente

_____ **2.** Ostpolitik

_____ **3.** Helsinki Accords

_____ **4.** Maastricht Treaty

_____ **5.** perestroika

_____ **6.** glasnost

_____ **7.** Lech Walesa

_____ **8.** Vaclav Havel

_____ **9.** World Trade Center

_____ **10.** Tom Ridge

a. easing of the strain between the United States and the Soviet Union

b. an agreement between 35 nations pledging economic and technological cooperation

c. restructuring

d. Germany's attempt to ease tensions with communist Eastern Europe

e. created the European Union

f. Polish electrician who lead the Solidarity movement

g. 110-story building attacked by terrorists

h. first head of Office of Homeland Security

i. president of Czechoslovakia

j. openness

FILL IN THE BLANK *(3 points each)* Choose from the following list to complete each of the statements below.

Colin Powell   Vietnamization   Helmut Kohl
Solidarity   Jimmy Carter   Commonwealth of
Meech Lake Accord   Brezhnev Doctrine   Independent States

1. During _____, American troops gradually withdrew from fighting, leaving South Vietnamese troops to finish the war.

2. Muslim militants took hostages at the American Embassy in Tehran, Iran, while

_____ was the president of the United States.

3. The _____ was an agreement that would have allowed Quebec to remain a "distinct society" within Canada.

4. After the September 11, 2001, terrorist attacks, Secretary of State

_____ led United States efforts to build an international coalition against terrorism.

5. _____ was the leader of Germany when the Berlin Wall came down.

6. The _____ stated that the Soviet Union would step in when any nation started moving away from communism.

7. The _____ was created after the breakup of the Soviet Union.

8. The trade union called _____ led to the end of communism in Poland.

TRUE/FALSE *(3 points each)* Mark each statement *T* if it is true or *F* if it is false.

_____ **1.** Ronald Reagan was impeached because of his involvement in the Iran-contra affair.

_____ **2.** The United States was able to balance the budget and strengthen the economy in the 1990s.

_____ **3.** The Official Languages Act made English the official language of Canada.

_____ **4.** Margaret Thatcher was the first Liberal Party woman elected to be prime minister of Great Britain.

_____ **5.** The Irish Republican Army helped the British regain control of the Falkland Islands.

_____ **6.** Leonid Brezhnev modernized factories, increased agricultural production, and solidified the Soviet economy.

_____ **7.** In 1991, calls for independence from Soviet republics led to the breakup of the Soviet Union.

_____ **8.** Russia used military force to keep the region of Chechnya from breaking away.

_____ **9.** Ethnic cleansing in Yugoslavia was an effort to remove Bosnian Serbs.

_____ **10.** Transition from communism to democracy in Czechoslovakia was peaceful.

Chapter 35, Chapter Test Form C, continued

IDENTIFICATION *(3 points each)* Match each phrase with the United States president with whom it is associated. Place the correct letter in the appropriate column on the chart.

   a. boycotted the Olympic Games

   b. Watergate

   c. governor of California

   d. resigned his office

   e. Iran-contra affair

   f. SALT

   g. impeached for lying to a grand jury

   h. governor of Arkansas

   i. Iran hostage crisis

   j. governor of Georgia

Richard Nixon	Jimmy Carter	Ronald Reagan	Bill Clinton
_____	_____	_____	_____
_____	_____	_____	_____
_____	_____	_____	

CHAPTER 36

Modern Chapter 27

Chapter Test Form C

The Modern World

MATCHING *(3 points each)* Place the letters of the descriptions next to the appropriate terms.

_____ 1. greenhouse effect

_____ 2. biodiversity

_____ 3. antibiotics

_____ 4. pop art

_____ 5. genetic code

_____ 6. acid rain

_____ 7. miniaturization

_____ 8. "ethnic cleansing"

_____ 9. urbanization

_____ 10. "theater of the absurd"

a. style of art using everyday objects

b. sequence of DNA that represents the structure of human life

c. form of theater used to present biting social commentary

d. movement of people from the countryside to cities

e. penicillin and similar substances that are used to treat or cure illnesses by killing or limiting bacterial growth

f. an example of human rights violation

g. naturally occurring variety of plants and animals in the environment

h. results from toxins in the air

i. theory that gases in the Earth's atmosphere warm the planet and keep heat from escaping

j. process of making machines and their parts lighter and smaller

FILL IN THE BLANK *(3 points each)* Choose from the following list to complete each of the statements below.

Jackson Pollock   Beats   Neil Armstrong
Martha Graham   Maya Angelou   *Challenger*
Federico Fellini   Yury Gagarin   Rachel Carson
Nelson Mandela

1. An American, _____, became a leader in modern dance.

2. One of America's foremost writers and poets, _____, explores racism and oppression of all kinds.

3. _____ was a leading abstract expressionist painter.

4. Italian director _____ made films that criticized political and social injustices.

Chapter 36, Chapter Test Form C, continued

5. The _____ were a group of writers who criticized wealthy citizens and their values.

6. The space shuttle _____ exploded shortly after lifting off in 1986.

7. _____ was the first man to walk on the moon.

8. _____ brought the issues of environmental pollution to the forefront with her book, *Silent Spring*.

9. _____ was elected by formerly powerless black majority in South Africa.

10. A Russian cosmonaut named _____ was the first person to travel in space.

TRUE/FALSE *(2 points each)* Mark each statement *T* if it is true or *F* if it is false.

_____ 1. Computer technology had an impact on many areas—including music and movies.

_____ 2. Iranian leaders issued a death sentence for Salman Rushdie because of the content of his novel *The Satanic Verses*.

_____ 3. More than half of American museums were founded before 1970.

_____ 4. The United States and Canada led the world in space exploration.

_____ 5. The Universal Declaration of Human Rights was difficult for the United Nations to enforce.

Chapter 36, Chapter Test Form C, continued

IDENTIFICATION *(5 points each)* Match each person or term with the category for which they are associated. Write the letter under the appropriate category.

a. ENIAC

b. "Chunnel"

c. Mikhail Baryshnikov

d. Alexander Fleming

e. "New Wave"

f. Arthur Miller

Arts	Science and Technology
_____	_____
_____	_____
_____	_____

UNIT 8
Modern Unit 6

Chapter Test Form C
The World Since 1945

MATCHING *(3 points each)* Place the letters of the descriptions next to the appropriate terms.

_____ **1.** petrodollars

_____ **2.** apartheid

_____ **3.** mixed economy

_____ **4.** zaibatsu

_____ **5.** cultural revolution

_____ **6.** contras

_____ **7.** inflation

_____ **8.** dissidents

_____ **9.** biodiversity

_____ **10.** miniaturization

_____ **11.** glasnost

_____ **12.** Solidarity

_____ **13.** monoculture

_____ **14.** Nürnberg trials

_____ **15.** Cold War

a. trials in which Nazi leaders were tried for war crimes

b. individuals who disagree with the government

c. reform, whose name means openness

d. a Nicaraguan rebel group, funded by the Reagan administration

e. process of redefining a people's customs, habits, and thoughts

f. system in which some businesses are owned by the government and some are owned by individuals

g. struggle of ideas and worldviews between communism and democracy

h. government policy whereby races are segregated

i. trade union that ended communism in Poland

j. huge Japanese industrial firms owned by powerful families

k. the variety of plants and animals that occur naturally in an environment

l. reliance on just one or two crops or minerals for exporting

m. a decrease in the value of money

n. oil profits

o. process in which machines and their parts were made lighter and smaller

FILL IN THE BLANK *(3 points each)* Choose from the following list to complete each of the statements below.

Ho Chi Minh	Jimmy Carter	Neil Armstrong
Nelson Mandela	Rachel Carson	Martin Luther King Jr.
Yasir Arafat	Fidel Castro	Nikita Khrushchev
Ferdinand Marcos		

Unit 8, Chapter Test Form C, continued

1. The leader of the Palestine Liberation Organization was

   _____.

2. _____ lifted many of Stalin's restrictions on the people of the
   Soviet Union.

3. _____ fought for, and was imprisoned for, South African
   independence.

4. The first man to walk on the moon was _____.

5. The American president _____ suffered foreign policy
   set-backs during his administration.

6. _____ led the Cuban revolution and installed himself as
   dictator of Cuba.

7. _____ was an American civil rights leader who called for an
   end to discrimination against African-Americans.

8. _____ wrote a book that exposed the damage being done to
   the environment by pesticides and pollution.

9. _____ declared Vietnamese independence in 1945 and
   instigated the Vietnam War by attempting to force communism on South Vietnam.

10. The corrupt Philippine president who was supported by the U.S. government was

    _____.

TRUE/FALSE *(2 points each)* Mark each statement *T* if it is true or *F* if it is false.

_____ **1.** Japan became a world power after World War II.

_____ **2.** The Truman Doctrine called for economic reform in Europe.

_____ **3.** Jimmy Carter is considered to have been one of the nation's most honorable
        presidents.

_____ **4.** The period after World War II is considered a time of great change and
        experimentation in the arts.

_____ **5.** The use of computer technology has led to many advances in medicine.

Unit 8, Chapter Test Form C, continued

IDENTIFICATION *(5 points each)* Find the name or phrase that describes an effect for each cause listed in the chart. Write each letter in the correct box.

   a. Camp David Accords

   b. Richard Nixon resigned.

   c. Marshall Plan

   d. The Universal Declaration of Human Rights is adopted by the UN.

   e. MacArthur Constitution

   f. Berlin Airlift

   g. Maastrict Treaty

   h. Paris Peace Accords

   i. Contadora Principles

   j. President George W. Bush declared war on terrorism.

Cause	Effect
Human rights abuses occurred during World War II.	**1.**
West Berlin was cut off from food and supplies.	**2.**
Europe was suffering great economic troubles.	**3.**
Japan's government needed to be demilitarized after the war.	**4.**
Americans wanted to end their involvement in Vietnam.	**5.**
Tensions grew between Israel and Egypt.	**6.**
Years of turmoil caused fighting in Central America.	**7.**
In the United States, hijacked planes hit the World Trade Center and the Pentagon.	**8.**
The *Washington Post* exposed the Watergate scandal.	**9.**
European nations wanted to find common trade practices.	**10.**

(EPILOGUE)

Chapter Test Form C

The Modern World

MATCHING *(2 points each)* Place the letters of the descriptions next to the appropriate names and terms.

_____ **1.** Louis XIV

_____ **2.** Enlightenment

_____ **3.** Otto von Bismark

_____ **4.** Hiroshima

_____ **5.** Tehran

_____ **6.** Yury Gagarin

_____ **7.** apartheid

_____ **8.** Taiwan

_____ **9.** Douglas MacArthur

_____ **10.** Persia

_____ **11.** New Deal

_____ **12.** Napoléon Bonaparte

_____ **13.** Reign of Terror

_____ **14.** mercantilism

_____ **15.** Restoration

a. Prussian statesman who rigidly controlled Prussia while strengthening the nation

b. period after the French Revolution when a small group tried to crush all political opposition

c. set of economic policies meant to help fight the Great Depression

d. period when scholars began to believe that logic and reason could explain human nature

e. South African system in which the black majority was forced to live as second-class citizens

f. city in Iran where the U.S. embassy was captured and Americans were held hostage

g. French monarch whose reign was the longest in French history

h. U.S. general who oversaw the re-organization of Japan after World War II

i. the European financial theory that said that colonies existed for use by the mother nation

j. the reign of Charles II, who was placed on the throne by the British people after the civil war

k. long lasting empire which ended in 1935 when it became the nation of Iran

l. French emperor who conquered most of Europe in the early 1800s

m. Soviet who was the first man to orbit Earth

n. island off the coast of China where the Chinese national government fled to after losing power

o. Japanese city destroyed by the United States with the atomic bomb

Epilogue, Chapter Test Form C, continued

FILL IN THE BLANK *(2 points each)* Choose from the following list to complete each of the statements below.

"Russification"   Bolsheviks   Warsaw Pact
Khmer Rouge   Boxer Rebellion   Nelson Mandela
United Nations   Colin Powell   Beat Generation
Mohandas Gandhi

1. The communist group in Cambodia responsible for over 1 million deaths was called

the _____.

2. The _____ is an organization of nations which attempts to manage international difficulties.

3. The _____ was an unsuccessful uprising of Chinese against their British oppressors.

4. The _____ overthrew the Russian czar and created the Soviet Union.

5. The _____ was a military defense agreement between communist nations during the Cold War.

6. A group of American writers and poets who were critical of the values of

mainstream America were the _____.

7. _____ was a political prisoner in South Africa, and later, its first president after the end of apartheid.

8. _____ led the movement against British occupation of India.

9. After the September 11, 2001, terrorist attacks, Secretary of State

_____ led U.S. efforts to build an international coalition against terrorism.

10. _____ was the process whereby non-Russians were forced to adopt Russian culture.

TRUE/FALSE *(2 points each)* Mark each statement *T* if it is true or *F* if it is false.

_____ **1.** Imperialism has led to dozens, if not hundreds, of conflicts and wars over the past 500 years.

_____ **2.** After Oliver Cromwell's death, his son Richard strengthened the English commonwealth.

_____ **3.** Charles II came to power during a period of time called the Restoration.

Epilogue, Chapter Test Form C, continued

_____ **4.** Adolf Hitler was the architect behind World War II who executed millions of non-Aryans because of his racist views.

_____ **5.** William III and Mary II led England to victory over the Dutch during the Glorious Revolution.

_____ **6.** Martin Luther King, Jr., was a leader of the Free South Africa movement.

_____ **7.** NAFTA was a trade agreement between Canada, the United States, and Mexico, which removed all trade barriers between the countries.

_____ **8.** The Philippines were a U.S. colony until they won their independence in 1946 after a ten-year guerilla war.

_____ **9.** The Canadian province of Quebec has instigated several unsuccessful civil wars in its effort to gain independence.

_____ **10.** Pakistan and India have remained on good terms since their split into separate Muslim and Hindu nations.

IDENTIFICATION *(3 points each)* Put the following events in order of their occurrence. Write the letter of each phrase next to the correct numbered space, from the earliest to the most recent.

a. World Trade Center and Pentagon hit by hijacked planes

b. Cuban Missile Crisis

c. the Great Depression

d. World War II

e. Bolsheviks create the Soviet Union in Russia

f. Napoléon becomes dictator of France

g. American Revolution

h. the Confederate States of America is formed

i. English Civil War

j. Restoration

1. _____   **6.** _____

2. _____   **7.** _____

3. _____   **8.** _____

4. _____   **9.** _____

5. _____   **10.** _____

(PROLOGUE)

Chapter Test Form C
The Ancient World

MATCHING *(3 points each)* Place the letters of the descriptions next to the appropriate terms.

_____ 1. civilization

_____ 2. Confucius

_____ 3. Homer

_____ 4. cultural diffusion

_____ 5. Siddhartha Gautama

_____ 6. Legalism

_____ 7. Socrates

_____ 8. Jesus

_____ 9. Daoism

_____ 10. caste system

a. division of society developed by ancient Indian civilizations

b. taught that people are selfish and must be controlled with harsh measures

c. Jewish teacher whose followers founded Christianity

d. developed a philosophy in China that stressed the importance of family, respect for one's elders, and respect for the past

e. developed a method of teaching through questioning

f. taught that people should think about the natural harmony of the world

g. wrote two Greek epics, the *Iliad* and the *Odyssey*

h. has the ability to produce extra food; has large cities or towns with some form of government; and people perform different jobs

i. founder of Buddhism

j. the spread of ideas and other aspects of a culture from one area to another

FILL IN THE BLANK *(3 points each)* Choose from the following list to complete each of the statements below.

cuneiform	Maya	Inca
karma	divison of labor	Mandate of Heaven
ethical monotheism	republic	

1. A _____ is a form of government in which voters elect their leaders.

2. Chinese emperors argued that they ruled under a _____, or a divinely granted rule.

3. The Sumerians developed a form of wedge-shaped writing called

_____, from the Latin word for "wedge."

Prologue, Chapter Test Form C, continued

4. Judaism is often called _____ because of its focus on right behavior.

5. At its height, the _____ Empire covered the present-day nations of Peru, Ecuador, Bolivia, and Chile.

6. One characteristic of a civilization, the _____ , involves people performing different jobs, instead of one person doing all kinds of work.

7. The Hindu idea of _____ describes the positive or negative force created by a person's actions.

8. The _____ civilization built pyramid-shaped temples to their gods and invented the only writing system in the Americas.

TRUE/FALSE *(2 points each)* Mark each statement *T* if it is true or *F* if it is false.

_____ **1.** The Qin and Han dynasties kept China united under a strong central government.

_____ **2.** The Neolithic agricultural revolution allowed early humans to live nomadic lives.

_____ **3.** The Hellenistic Age was characterized by general disunity among the Greek city-states.

_____ **4.** The Lydians were the first people to make coined money.

_____ **5.** Mansa Mūsā was a great Sumerian ruler.

_____ **6.** The Four Noble Truths and the Eightfold Path are elements of Hinduism.

_____ **7.** Augustus Caesar's rule is seen as the end of the Roman Republic and the beginning of the Roman Empire.

_____ **8.** The Aztec people performed sacrifices for their gods.

Prologue, Chapter Test Form C, continued

IDENTIFICATION *(5 points each)* Determine which of the following statements best describes each of the civilizations below. Write the letter of each statement in the appropriate box.

a. Hammurabi

b. Menes

c. Alexander the Great

d. King 'Ēzānā

e. origins of the alphabet we use today

f. Amenhotep IV

g. Julius Caesar

h. pope

i. Swahili

j. Socrates

Greece	Rome	Fertile Crescent	Africa	Egypt
_____	_____	_____	_____	_____
_____	_____	_____	_____	_____
_____	_____	_____	_____	_____
_____	_____	_____	_____	_____
_____	_____	_____	_____	_____
_____	_____	_____	_____	_____

Chapter 1

FORM C
Matching
1. h	6. f
2. g	7. b
3. a	8. d
4. j	9. i
5. e	10. c

Fill in the Blank
1. anthropologist	6. division of labor
2. limited evidence	7. hunter-gatherers
3. Ice Age	8. artisans
4. Neanderthals	9. Bronze Age
5. Neolithic agricultural revolution	10. nomads

True/False
1. F
2. T
3. T
4. F
5. F

Identification
Column 1	Column 2
a	c
b	d
f	e

Chapter 2

FORM C
Matching
1. g	9. d
2. m	10. h
3. i	11. f
4. e	12. l
5. j	13. b
6. n	14. o
7. c	15. k
8. a	

Fill in the Blank
1. Great Sphinx
2. Twelve Tribes of Israel
3. Rosetta Stone
4. Zoroaster
5. Nile River

6. Fertile Crescent
7. Sumerians
8. scribes

True/False
1. F	5. T
2. T	6. T
3. F	7. T
4. T	8. F

Identification
Column 1	Column 2	Column 3
b	c	a
f	e	d
i	g	h
	j	

Chapter 3

FORM C
Matching
1. b	6. h
2. a	7. d
3. c	8. e
4. g	9. j
5. i	10. f

Fill in the Blank
1. Vedas	6. Brahmins
2. suttee	7. monsoons
3. Aśoka	8. Hinduism
4. Buddhism	9. raja
5. polygyny	10. epics

True/False
1. F
2. T
3. T
4. F
5. T

Identification
Left Circle	Middle	Right Circle
a	b	c
d	e	f

Chapter 4

FORM C
Matching
1. c
2. j
3. f
4. b
5. a
6. g
7. e
8. h
9. d
10. i

Fill in the Blank
1. leveling
2. Great Wall of China
3. civil service
4. dikes
5. animism
6. Xia
7. Buddhism
8. calligraphy
9. *Analects*
10. Five Classics

True/False
1. F
2. T
3. F
4. T
5. T

Identification
Column 1	Column 2	Column 3
b	d	a
c	e	f
h	i	g
		j

Unit 1

FORM C
Matching
1. c
2. g
3. i
4. d
5. b
6. f
7. e
8. h
9. j
10. a

Fill in the Blank
1. animism
2. barter
3. artifacts
4. polytheism
5. money economy
6. civilization
7. caste system
8. cultural diffusion
9. reincarnation
10. inoculation

True/False
1. T
2. F
3. T
4. T
5. F

Identification
Column 1	Column 2	Column 3
c	a	b
e	d	f
i	g	h
		j

Chapter 5

FORM C
Matching
1. d
2. f
3. c
4. h
5. j
6. e
7. i
8. a
9. g
10. b

Fill in the Blank
1. agora
2. Minoan
3. aristocracies
4. popular government
5. representative democracy
6. direct democracy
7. pedagogue
8. archons
9. Battle of Marathon
10. Battle of Thermopylae

True/False
1. F
2. T
3. F
4. F
5. T

Identification
Column 1	Column 2
a	b
d	c
e	f
g	i
h	j

Chapter 6

FORM C
Matching
1. f
2. k
3. a
4. m
5. l
6. h
7. b
8. j
9. c
10. d
11. e
12. n
13. g
14. i
15. o

Fill in the Blank
1. orator
2. philosophy
3. aristocracy
4. drama
5. phalanxes

True/False
1. F
2. F
3. F
4. T
5. T
6. T
7. F
8. T
9. T
10. F

Identification
Column 1	Column 2
b	a
d	c
f	e
h	g
i	j

Chapter 7

FORM C
Matching
1. g
2. l
3. d
4. e
5. k
6. m
7. f
8. c
9. j
10. o
11. b
12. n
13. i
14. a
15. h

Fill in the Blank
1. veto
2. dictator
3. aqueducts
4. gladiators
5. martyrs
6. pope
7. inflation
8. rabbis
9. checks and balances
10. censors

True/False
1. T
2. T
3. F
4. F
5. T

Organization
1. d
2. f
3. a
4. e
5. c
6. b

Chapter 8

FORM C
Matching
1. d
2. f
3. e
4. c
5. j
6. a
7. b
8. g
9. h
10. i

Fill in the Blank
1. Great Rift Valley
2. Tunka Manin
3. Sonni´Alī
4. Mohammed I Askia
5. Sahara Desert
6. King ´Ezānā
7. Mansa Mūsā
8. Great Zimbabwe
9. Shona
10. Mount Kilimanjaro

True/False

1. F
2. F
3. T
4. T
5. T

Identification

Column 1		Column 2
b	→	f
d	→	a
e	→	c

Chapter 9

FORM C
Matching

1. c
2. g
3. d
4. f
5. e
6. j
7. i
8. b
9. a
10. h

Fill in the Blank

1. Quetzalcoatl
2. Aztec
3. Hohokam
4. Mississippians
5. Pueblo
6. Cahokia
7. Inca
8. Maya
9. Olmec
10. Toltec

True/False

1. T
2. T
3. F
4. T
5. T

Organization

Column 1	Column 2
f	d
b	e
c	a

Unit 2

FORM C
Matching

1. g
2. b
3. j
4. n
5. e
6. o
7. h
8. a
9. c
10. l
11. i
12. m
13. k
14. d
15. f

Fill in the Blank

1. Philip II of Macedon
2. terracing
3. gold-for-salt exchange
4. checks and balances
5. Minoan
6. Julio-Claudian Emperors
7. oracles
8. Quechua
9. democracy
10. Beringia

True/False

1. T
2. F
3. T
4. T
5. T

Identification

Column 1	Column 2	Column 3
c	b	a
e	f	d

Chapter 10 (Modern Chapter 1)

FORM C
Matching

1. j
2. g
3. h
4. a
5. i
6. b
7. f
8. d
9. c
10. e

Fill in the Blank
1. Slavs
2. Methodius
3. Hagia Sophia
4. Pravda Russkia
5. Greek fire
6. Iconoclastic Controversy
7. Ottoman Turks
8. Vladimir I
9. third Rome
10. Justinian Code

True/False
1. T
2. F
3. T
4. T
5. T

Identification

Column 1	Column 2
b	a
c	e
d	f

Chapter 11
(Modern Chapter 2)

FORM C
Matching
1. h
2. d
3. f
4. g
5. a
6. j
7. c
8. b
9. e
10. i

Fill in the Blank
1. mosques
2. Islam
3. Five Pillars of Islam
4. Qur'an
5. Kaaba
6. hijrah
7. Tāriq
8. al-Rāzī
9. Moors
10. *The Thousand and One Nights*

True/False
1. F
2. F
3. T
4. T
5. T

Identification
1. b
2. e
3. d
4. f
5. a
6. c

Chapter 12
(Modern Chapter 3)

FORM C
Matching
1. f
2. c
3. j
4. b
5. d
6. g
7. a
8. i
9. e
10. h

Fill in the Blank
1. footbinding
2. Golden Horde
3. *kamikaze*
4. *Diamond Sutra*
5. tea ceremony
6. *The Tale of Genji*
7. shogun
8. Grand Canal
9. Du Fu
10. samurai

True/False
1. F
2. T
3. T
4. F
5. F

Identification

Column 1	Column 2
b	a
c	d
f	e

Chapter 13
(Modern Chapter 4)

FORM C
Matching
1. j	**9.** a
2. n	**10.** k
3. b	**11.** o
4. c	**12.** m
5. g	**13.** d
6. h	**14.** f
7. l	**15.** i
8. e	

Fill in the Blank
1. monasticism	**6.** Innocent III
2. Saint Patrick	**7.** Charlemagne
3. Inquisition	**8.** Vikings
4. Thomas Becket	**9.** Saint Benedict
5. Magna Carta	**10.** Gregory VI

True/False
1. F
2. T
3. T
4. F
5. T

Identification
d
e
c
a
b

Chapter 14
(Modern Chapter 5)

FORM C
Matching
1. f	**9.** k
2. c	**10.** e
3. j	**11.** m
4. g	**12.** b
5. i	**13.** h
6. o	**14.** a
7. l	**15.** d
8. n	

Fill in the Blank
1. John Wycliffe
2. Dante Alighieri
3. Thomas Aquinas
4. Hundred Years' War
5. Geoffrey Chaucer
6. Joan of Arc
7. Babylonian Captivity
8. War of the Roses

True/False
1. T	**5.** F
2. T	**6.** T
3. F	**7.** T
4. T	**8.** F

Identification
Column 1	Column 2
c	a
e	b
f	d

Unit 3 (Modern Unit 1)

FORM C
Matching
1. i	**9.** e
2. g	**10.** n
3. m	**11.** l
4. j	**12.** k
5. a	**13.** b
6. c	**14.** f
7. o	**15.** h
8. d	

Fill in the Blank
1. steppe	**6.** domestic system
2. heresy	**7.** *kamikaze*
3. feudalism	**8.** samurai
4. chivalry	**9.** jihad
5. mosques	**10.** scholasticism

True/False
1. T
2. T
3. T
4. F
5. F

Identification

Column 1	Column 2	Column 3
e	a	b
g	f	c
h	i	d
j		

Chapter 15
(Modern Chapter 6)

FORM C
Matching

1.	e	**6.**	i
2.	f	**7.**	c
3.	j	**8.**	h
4.	g	**9.**	b
5.	a	**10.**	d

Fill in the Blank
1. humanists
2. sects
3. Leonardo da Vinci
4. Michelangelo
5. Desiderius Erasmus

True/False

1.	T	**6.**	F
2.	F	**7.**	F
3.	F	**8.**	T
4.	T	**9.**	F
5.	T	**10.**	T

Identification

Column 1	Column 2
b	a
d	c
f	e
g	h
j	i

Chapter 16
(Modern Chapter 7)

FORM C
Matching

1.	j	**6.**	b
2.	d	**7.**	e
3.	o	**8.**	a
4.	n	**9.**	g
5.	f	**10.**	m

11.	l	**14.**	k
12.	h	**15.**	c
13.	i		

Fill in the Blank
1. heliocentric theory
2. joint-stock company
3. favorable balance of trade
4. tariff
5. scientific method
6. alchemists
7. mercantilism
8. triangular trade
9. subsidy
10. guerrilla warfare

True/False
1. T
2. F
3. T
4. F
5. T

Identification
1. b
2. c
3. d
4. a
5. e

Chapter 17
(Modern Chapter 8)

FORM C
Matching

1.	g	**6.**	a
2.	i	**7.**	e
3.	j	**8.**	h
4.	f	**9.**	c
5.	d	**10.**	b

Fill in the Blank
1. East India Tea Company
2. Opium War
3. Oda Nobunaga
4. Tokugawa Ieyasu
5. Matthew Perry
6. Toyotomi Hideyoshi
7. Hsüan-yeh
8. Great Wall of China

True/False

1. T	5. T
2. T	6. F
3. F	7. T
4. T	8. F

Identification

1. b	4. c
2. d	5. a
3. e	6. f

Chapter 18 (Modern Chapter 9)

FORM C
Matching

1. g	6. d
2. c	7. j
3. f	8. a
4. i	9. e
5. h	10. b

Fill in the Blank

1. kizilbash
2. millets
3. reaya
4. Janissaries
5. ghazis

True/False

1. T	6. F
2. T	7. T
3. F	8. T
4. F	9. F
5. T	10. T

Identification

Column 1	Column 2	Column 3
a	f	g
i	e	d
c	h	b

Unit 4 (Modern Unit 2)

FORM C
Matching

1. e	6. b
2. g	7. j
3. f	8. c
4. i	9. a
5. h	10. d

Fill in the Blank

1. Treaty of Kangawa
2. Reformation
3. humanists
4. ghazis
5. guerrilla warfare
6. scientific method
7. White Lotus Rebellion
8. mercantilism
9. reaya
10. Flemish School

True/False

1. F	6. T
2. T	7. F
3. T	8. F
4. T	9. T
5. T	10. F

Identification

Left Circle	Middle Circle	Right Circle
a	h	i
d	e	c
f	j	g
	b	

Chapter 19 (Modern Chapter 10)

FORM C
Matching

1. e
2. d
3. a
4. b
5. c

Fill in the Blank

1. intendants
2. divine right of kings
3. balance of power
4. gentry
5. Pragmatic Sanction
6. Diplomatic Revolution
7. Spanish Armada
8. Puritans
9. burgesses
10. service nobility

True/False
1. F	**6.** F
2. F	**7.** T
3. T	**8.** T
4. T	**9.** T
5. T	**10.** F

Identification
Column 1	Column 2
a	e
d	c
f	b

Chapter 20
(Modern Chapter 11)

FORM C
Matching
1. g	**9.** i
2. n	**10.** m
3. k	**11.** l
4. h	**12.** f
5. c	**13.** j
6. e	**14.** a
7. o	**15.** b
8. d	

Fill in the Blank
1. Petition of Right
2. Navigation Act of 1651
3. Rump Parliament
4. Long Parliament
5. Habeas Corpus Act
6. prime minister
7. sea dogs
8. mercantilism
9. federal system of government
10. Bill of Rights

True/False
1. T	**6.** F
2. F	**7.** F
3. T	**8.** T
4. T	**9.** T
5. F	**10.** T

Identification
1. c	**6.** d
2. i	**7.** h
3. b	**8.** f
4. j	**9.** g
5. e	**10.** a

Chapter 21
(Modern Chapter 12)

FORM C
Matching
1. g	**6.** e
2. b	**7.** a
3. f	**8.** j
4. c	**9.** d
5. i	**10.** h

Fill in the Blank
1. bourgeoisie
2. Louis XVI
3. émigrés
4. universal manhood suffrage
5. Reign of Terror
6. Directory
7. scorched-earth policy
8. legitimacy
9. liberalism
10. reactionaries

True/False
1. F
2. T
3. T
4. T
5. F

Identification
Column 1	Column 2	Column 3
a	b	c
f	d	e
i	h	g

Unit 5 (Modern Unit 3)

FORM C
Matching
1. h	**6.** b
2. c	**7.** e
3. i	**8.** g
4. f	**9.** a
5. j	**10.** d

Fill in the Blank
1. Catherine the Great
2. John Locke
3. Benjamin Franklin
4. Napoléon Bonaparte
5. Maria Theresa
6. Oliver Cromwell
7. Sir Francis Drake
8. John Cabot

True/False
1. T
2. F
3. T
4. F
5. T
6. F
7. F
8. T

Identification

Column 1	Column 2
c	a
e	b
f	d
g	h
j	i

Chapter 22
(Modern Chapter 13)

FORM C
Matching
1. c
2. g
3. a
4. j
5. e
6. b
7. f
8. h
9. d
10. i

Fill in the Blank
1. vulcanization
2. mechanization
3. tenements
4. middle class
5. capitalism
6. interchangeable parts
7. corporations
8. strike
9. collective bargaining
10. socialism

True/False
1. F
2. T
3. T
4. F
5. F

Identification

Column 1	Column 2
d	e
g	f

Column 3	Column 4
a	b
h	c
j	i

Chapter 23
(Modern Chapter 14)

FORM C
Matching
1. c
2. g
3. d
4. b
5. f
6. j
7. k
8. m
9. i
10. o
11. n
12. h
13. l
14. e
15. a

Fill in the Blank
1. psychiatry
2. suburbs
3. romanticism
4. aerodynamics
5. genetics
6. dynamo
7. emigration
8. social Darwinism
9. bobbies
10. petroleum

True/False
1. F
2. T
3. T
4. T
5. F
6. F
7. T
8. F
9. T
10. T

Identification

Column 1	Column 2	Column 3
d	b	a
f	e	c

Chapter 24
(Modern Chapter 15)

FORM C
Matching

1. g		**6.** h
2. f		**7.** d
3. c		**8.** b
4. a		**9.** i
5. j		**10.** e

Fill in the Blank

1. suffragettes
2. sectionalism
3. anarchists
4. coalitions
5. haciendas

True/False

1. F		**6.** T
2. T		**7.** T
3. T		**8.** F
4. F		**9.** T
5. F		**10.** F

Identification

Column 1	Column 2
a	b
g	e
l	i
o	n

Column 3	Column 4
c	d
f	h
k	j
m	

Chapter 25
(Modern Chapter 16)

FORM C
Matching

1. f		**6.** e
2. c		**7.** b
3. i		**8.** d
4. a		**9.** j
5. h		**10.** g

Fill in the Blank

1. risorgimento
2. Carbonari
3. kaiser
4. Junkers
5. Kulturkampf
6. Emancipation Edict
7. People's Will
8. pogroms
9. Treaty of San Stefano
10. Balkan League

True/False

1. T
2. F
3. F
4. F
5. T

Identification

Column 1	Column 2
d	c
i	e
	g

Column 3	Column 4
a	b
f	j
h	

Chapter 26
(Modern Chapter 17)

FORM C
Matching

1. a		**6.** f
2. c		**7.** d
3. j		**8.** i
4. g		**9.** e
5. b		**10.** h

Fill in the Blank

1. Fashoda crisis
2. assimilation
3. Meiji Restoration
4. Sino-Japanese War
5. buffer state

True/False

1. F
2. T
3. F
4. T
5. F
6. F
7. T
8. T
9. F
10. T

Identification

Column 1	Column 2
e	i
f	
c	g

Column 3	Column 4
d	b
a	j
	h

Unit 6 (Modern Unit 4)

FORM C
Matching

1. f
2. h
3. g
4. e
5. i
6. j
7. d
8. l
9. k
10. m
11. c
12. b
13. o
14. n
15. a

Fill in the Blank

1. Florence Nightengale
2. J.P. Morgan
3. Emancipation Edict
4. Jane Addams
5. Thomas Edison
6. social Darwinism
7. Karl Marx
8. Fashoda crisis

True/False

1. F
2. T
3. T
4. F
5. F
6. T
7. T
8. F

Identification

Column 1	Column 2
e	c
i	d
	h

Column 3	Column 4
a	b
f	g
	j

Chapter 27 (Modern Chapter 18)

FORM C
Matching

1. c
2. h
3. f
4. a
5. j
6. b
7. e
8. i
9. d
10. g

Fill in the Blank

1. militarism
2. ultimatum
3. belligerents
4. total war
5. Bolshevik
6. Fourteen Points
7. Big Four
8. League of Nations

True/False

1. T
2. T
3. T
4. F
5. F
6. F
7. T
8. F

Identification

Column 1	Column 2
c	a
d	b
f	e
h	g
i	j

Chapter 28
(Modern Chapter 19)

FORM C
Matching
1. i
2. h
3. a
4. g
5. f
6. e
7. c
8. b
9. j
10. d

Fill in the Blank
1. cubism
2. influenza pandemic
3. market speculations
4. New Deal
5. purge
6. Rome-Berlin Axis
7. Black Tuesday
8. Easter Rising
9. Black Shirts
10. command economy

True/False
1. T
2. T
3. F
4. T
5. T
6. F
7. T
8. T

Identification
Column 1	Column 2
d	c
g	h

Column 3	Column 4
a	b
f	e

Chapter 29
(Modern Chapter 20)

FORM C
Matching
1. d
2. a
3. e
4. c
5. b
6. f
7. h
8. g

Fill in the Blank
1. Wafd Party
2. Balfour Declaration
3. passive resistance
4. Open Door Policy
5. Boxer Rebellion
6. Kuomintang
7. Treaty of Portsmouth
8. militarism
9. Good Neighbor Policy
10. nitrates

True/False
1. F
2. T
3. F
4. T
5. F
6. F
7. F
8. T
9. F
10. T

Identification
Column 1	Column 2
d	b
e	c

Column 3	Column 4
f	a
h	g

Chapter 30
(Modern Chapter 21)

FORM C
Matching
1. b
2. f
3. i
4. g
5. h
6. j
7. c
8. a
9. e
10. d

Fill in the Blank
1. Francisco Franco
2. Anti-Comintern Pact
3. Winston Churchill
4. Charles de Gaulle
5. V-E Day
6. Heinrich Himmler
7. V-J Day
8. Bataan Death March

True/False

1. F	6. F
2. T	7. T
3. T	8. T
4. F	9. T
5. F	10. T

Identification

Column 1	Column 2
j	b
d	g
h	k
f	e
c	l

Unit 7 (Modern Unit 5)

FORM C
Matching

1. c	6. h
2. d	7. i
3. g	8. a
4. f	9. e
5. j	10. b

Fill in the Blank

1. nitrates
2. market speculations
3. blitzkrieg
4. isolationists
5. armistice
6. total war
7. passive resistance
8. command economy
9. appeasement
10. economic sanctions

True/False

1. T	6. F
2. T	7. T
3. F	8. F
4. F	9. T
5. T	10. T

Identification

Column 1	Column 2
c	a
d	b
e	f
h	g
i	j

Chapter 31 (Modern Chapter 22)

FORM C
Matching

1. i	6. b
2. e	7. f
3. h	8. d
4. j	9. c
5. a	10. g

Fill in the Blank

1. Nürnberg trials
2. Security Council
3. veto power
4. Cold War
5. Cuban missile crisis
6. containment
7. Berlin Airlift
8. welfare state

True/False

1. F	5. T
2. T	6. F
3. T	7. T
4. T	8. T

Identification

Column 1

1. d
2. c
3. b
4. e
5. a

Chapter 32 (Modern Chapter 23)

FORM C
Matching

1. e	6. b
2. a	7. d
3. c	8. j
4. h	9. f
5. g	10. i

Fill in the Blank

1. Muslim League
2. "Quit India"
3. mixed economy
4. Great Leap Forward
5. Cultural Revolution
6. MacArthur Constitution
7. zaibatsu
8. Geneva Accord
9. ASEAN
10. Four Tigers

True/False

1. T
2. F
3. T
4. T
5. F

Identification

Column 1	Column 2	Column 3
a	e	c
i	f	g
m	o	j

Column 4	Column 5
h	b
l	d
n	k

Chapter 33
(Modern Chapter 24)

TEST FORM C
Matching

1. d
2. f
3. a
4. b
5. e
6. g
7. h
8. c

Fill in the Blank

1. Pan-African movement
2. Kikuyu
3. apartheid
4. kibbutz
5. Suez Crisis
6. Six Day War
7. intifada
8. petrodollars

True/False

1. T   6. F
2. F   7. T
3. F   8. T
4. T   9. F
5. T   10. F

Identification

Column 1	Column 2
1. b	4. e
2. a	5. d
3. j	

Column 3	Column 4
6. h	9. i
7. g	10. c
8. f	

Chapter 34
(Modern Chapter 25)

TEST FORM C
Matching

1. c
2. a
3. e
4. b
5. d

Fill in the Blank

1. multinational corporations
2. monoculture
3. inflation
4. contras
5. Contadora Principles
6. dissidents
7. Grenada
8. Brazilian Miracle
9. "dirty war"
10. Falkland Islands

True/False

1. T   6. F
2. T   7. F
3. F   8. T
4. T   9. F
5. F   10. F

Identification

Left circle	Middle	Right Circle
a	b	g
d	c	i
f	e	j
	h	

Chapter 35
(Modern Chapter 26)

FORM C
Matching

1. a		**6.** j
2. d		**7.** f
3. b		**8.** i
4. e		**9.** g
5. c		**10.** h

Fill in the Blank

1. Vietnamization
2. Jimmy Carter
3. Meech Lake Accord
4. Colin Powell
5. Helmut Kohl
6. Brezhnev Doctrine
7. Commonwealth of Independent States
8. Solidarity

True/False

1. F		**6.** F
2. T		**7.** T
3. F		**8.** T
4. F		**9.** F
5. F		**10.** T

Identification

Column 1	Column 2
b	a
d	j
f	i

Column 3	Column 4
c	g
e	h

Chapter 36
(Modern Chapter 27)

FORM C
Matching

1. i		**6.** h
2. g		**7.** j
3. e		**8.** f
4. a		**9.** d
5. b		**10.** c

Fill in the Blank

1. Martha Graham
2. Maya Angelou
3. Jackson Pollock
4. Federico Fellini
5. Beats
6. *Challenger*
7. Neil Armstrong
8. Rachel Carson
9. Nelson Mandela
10. Yury Gagarin

True/False

1. T
2. T
3. F
4. F
5. T

Identification

Column 1	Column 2
c	a
e	b
f	d

Unit 8 (Modern Unit 6)

FORM C
Matching

1. n		**9.** k
2. h		**10.** o
3. f		**11.** c
4. j		**12.** i
5. e		**13.** l
6. d		**14.** a
7. m		**15.** g
8. b		

Fill in the Blank
1. Yasir Arafat
2. Nikita Khrushchev
3. Nelson Mandela
4. Neil Armstrong
5. Jimmy Carter
6. Fidel Castro
7. Martin Luther King Jr.
8. Rachel Carson
9. Ho Chi Minh
10. Ferdinand Marcos

True/False
1. T
2. F
3. T
4. T
5. T

Identification
1. d
2. f
3. c
4. e
5. h
6. a
7. i
8. j
9. b
10. g

Epilogue

FORM C
Matching
1. g
2. d
3. a
4. o
5. f
6. m
7. e
8. n
9. h
10. k
11. c
12. l
13. b
14. i
15. j

Fill in the Blank
1. Khmer Rouge
2. United Nations
3. Boxer Rebellion
4. Bolsheviks
5. Warsaw Pact
6. Beat Generation
7. Nelson Mandela
8. Mohandas Gandhi
9. Colin Powell
10. "Russification"

True/False
1. T
2. F
3. T
4. T
5. F
6. F
7. T
8. F
9. F
10. F

Identification
1. i
2. j
3. g
4. f
5. h
6. e
7. c
8. d
9. b
10. a

Prologue

FORM C
Matching
1. h
2. d
3. g
4. j
5. i
6. b
7. e
8. c
9. f
10. a

Fill in the Blank
1. republic
2. Mandate of Heaven
3. cuneiform
4. ethical monotheism
5. Inca
6. division of labor
7. karma
8. Maya

True/False
1. T
2. F
3. F
4. T
5. F
6. F
7. T
8. T

Identification

Column 1	Column 2	Column 3
c	g	a
j	h	e

Column 4	Column 5
d	b
i	f

CURRICULUM